COINS HAVE TALES TO TELL

COINS HAVE TALES TO TELL

TO TELL

The Story of American Coins

FRANCES WILLIAMS BROWIN

J. B. LIPPINCOTT COMPANY

Philadelphia   *New York*

Copyright © 1966 by Frances Williams Browin

PRINTED IN THE UNITED STATES OF AMERICA

Library of Congress Catalog Card Number 66-10901

Fourth Printing

Typography by Tere LoPrete

For permission to use the pictures on the following pages the author gratefully credits:

THE AMERICAN NUMISMATIC SOCIETY: 2, 3, 5, 8, 10, 13 (top), 14, 15, 16, 22, 23, 25, 26, 28, 29, 31, 32, 33, 36, 37, 38, 42, 43, 50, 53, 59, 61, 62, 63, 65, 67, 68, 70, 71, 73, 74, 75, 77 (left), 78, 80, 82, 83, 87, 93, 94, 99, 100, 101, 102, 106, 108, 111, 115, 120, 121, and 122

BUREAU OF THE MINT—TREASURY DEPARTMENT: 46

THE CHASE MANHATTAN BANK MONEY MUSEUM: 13 (bottom), 77 (right), and 113

THE HISTORICAL SOCIETY OF PENNSYLVANIA: 51

FOR BEVERLY

CONTENTS

Chapter One

COLLECTING HISTORY

Coins bring history to life. Somehow when you read about George Washington he seems too far away and long ago to be quite real. But then a coin collector shows you his prized 1794 silver dollar, asking you please to handle it with care. As you hold it timidly by its edges you marvel that its date, its eagle, and its bust of a mussy-haired Liberty are still almost as clear as they must have been back in the days when Washington was alive.

Suddenly it occurs to you that just possibly this coin might be one that the first President himself used for paying a servant or a hairdresser or for buying theater tickets. Whatever the precious dollar's past, there is one thing about it that is certain: it was handled and valued by men and women who lived and worked when the United States was new.

Once you start on this line of thought you will find it hard ever

1. 1794 silver dollar

again to look on coins merely as money made of metal. For example, if you come upon a large-sized cent coined in 1820 you are likely to start thinking that this was made at about the time Abe Lincoln was earning his first pennies. Could it be . . . ?

Whether or not that particular copper piece could be one that the boy Abe actually touched, there can be little doubt that he **did** touch others exactly like it. And as you look upon this coin and others of its era the past seems closer than it did before. People die, and most of their houses and possessions disappear, but long after they are gone their coins remain to form a link with the past.

Men like to build great monuments to themselves and to their heroes, but oddly enough the everyday coins they use in their marketplaces are far more likely to endure through the centuries than are those mighty monuments. Coins have long survived the vast marvels they commemorated. Ours to see for the asking in museums or in coin collections are small metal likenesses of such rulers as Alexander the Great and Julius Caesar and of such vanished wonders as the huge gold-and-ivory statue of Zeus at Olympia or the Temple of Diana at Ephesus. The rulers and the temples are gone, but miniature images of them endure on coins minted two thousand and more years ago.

Many civilizations have come and gone since the seventh century B.C., when coins first came into use. When you read about archeologists discovering remains of one of these, you usually see something like this: "Pottery and coins found by the diggers indicate that this settlement was active in the —th century." It is partly from such coins, unearthed in various treasure troves and ruins, that we have gained much of our knowledge about how people lived and thought a couple of millenniums ago. From pictures and inscriptions on coins we know for sure that in ancient Greece and Rome people really did pay homage to such gods as Jupiter, Apollo, Athena, and Hercules, or that the Emperor Nero had three or four chins.

Even the Bible takes on new meaning when we find ourselves looking upon coins mentioned in its pages. The "tribute penny," the "widow's mite," and the "thirty pieces of silver" which Judas received for his betrayal of Jesus are not just words on a printed page —they are actual coins which you still can see today. Numismatists (authorities on coins) tell us that the tribute penny was probably a Roman denarius, and the widow's mite a tiny bronze Judean lepton, while the thirty pieces of silver were almost certainly tetradrachms minted by the ancient lands of Antioch and Tyre. If it seems odd that the Judea of Christ's time made use of coins from so many different places, it is no odder than the hodgepodge that passed for money in our own country's colonial days. How those early Americans finally worked their way out of their financial mess is told in the following chapters, which present the story of our coinage in terms of American history.

These glimpses into history are, in fact, one of the many reasons

2. *Roman denarius of Tiberius*

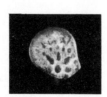

3. *Bronze lepton of Judea*

4. *Silver tetradrachm of Antioch,* A.D. 5

why people go in for coin collecting. Some say they are buying coins as an investment, and certainly that can be a perfectly good reason. A good example of this "investment" idea is to be found in "proofs" (uncirculated coins minted with specially polished dies on perfect metal blanks). If you spend several dollars for a set of brilliant proofs as soon as they are issued and then hold on to them for ten years or so you are almost certain to find them worth much more than you paid for them. And, of course, coins are a splendid investment if you are lucky enough to get hold of something that turns out to be such a "premium piece" as a rare 1909 Lincoln cent bearing the tiny initials "VDB" or a piece on which the date of one year has been struck over that of another.

Chances are, however, that coin collectors who follow their hobby as a way of making money are far fewer in number than those who do it just for sheer fun or because they admire coins as miniature works of art (as they certainly are). You need not even be a serious collector to know the thrill of reliving history through coins, and in the process you can find the answers to any number of interesting questions.

For instance, what did the Civil War's Union soldiers spend when they were on furlough? They spent silver coins from half dimes to dollars, all showing a full-length figure of Liberty, sitting with her robes flowing around her. They spent little silver three-cent pieces with a six-pointed star on one side and a Roman numeral III on the other. And they spent three or four different kinds of copper or bronze cents, with a few bronze two-centers adding to the mixture during the war's last year or so. One thing they certainly did *not* spend, however, was nickels, for nickels were not minted until 1866.

What sort of pennies did Thomas Alva Edison use for making change when he was a newsboy on the Grand Trunk Railroad in the years around 1860? Actually, he did not use pennies at all, for there never has been a United States coin named the penny; what we so commonly call that (even in this book) is properly, of course, a cent. The cents that filled newsboy Edison's pockets could have been the little "flying eagles" of 1856 to 1858. Some of them, perhaps, were the bulky Liberty-head coppers that served as cents for more than sixty years before the flying eagles. Most likely of all, however, they were the newer pieces known as "Indian heads," just getting well started on their fifty-year career, which lasted till Abraham Lincoln, a century after his birth, took the Indian's place. (The joke about the "Indian-head" coins is that their name is quite as inaccurate as the term "penny." The portrait they bear, say authorities, is not of an Indian but of a white girl in an Indian bonnet.)

If you are a coin collector you probably have formed the habit of taking a careful look, whenever possible, at every coin you handle. Let's say that, spreading the contents of your pocket or change purse on a table, you find there two quarters, five dimes, two nickels, and seven cents: $1.17 in all.

Chances are that $1.17 is about all they are worth in cash. But coins do not need premium values to be interesting. Consider, for instance, this cent dated 1943. Instead of the usual copper color it has a blackened look like a piece of old steel. As a matter of fact, it *is* steel, for when it was minted, during World War II, copper was scarce.

5. *1943 steel cent*

Let's examine the nickels. The one stamped "1945" is an unusual piece, for that was one of the years when five-cent pieces contained no nickel whatever. Even in the best of times the coin we call a nickel is made of a mixture of copper and nickel, but wartime needs from 1942 to 1945 made nickel so scarce that five-cent pieces were an alloy or mixture of copper, silver, and a form of steel called manganese. (Two or more metals mixed together are stronger than the metals in their pure form, so coins are almost always made of alloys.)

These part-silver nickels were confusing, for two nickels are supposed to equal one dime in value, yet the amount of silver in two wartime nickels was considerably greater than that in a dime. Fortunately, by 1946 the nickel shortage was about over, so silver no longer was used in five-cent pieces. Those minted from '42 to '45 are still too plentiful to have any extra value, but it seems safe to prophesy that some day they will be valued at much more than five cents.

Also included in that pile of change we have been examining are five dimes and two quarters. Two of the dimes are worth a special look, for they are of successive years, 1945 and 1946, yet they are very different. That of 1945 bears on its face a Liberty head looking so much like the common image of that fleet-footed ancient deity named Mercury that people usually call it (incorrectly) the "Mercury dime." The '46 one, however, shows instead of Liberty-Mercury a profile of Franklin D. Roosevelt. There was a good reason for that change: President Roosevelt had died in office the preceding year, and the new dime was designed as a memorial to him.

How about your two quarters? Being dated 1951 and 1958, they are not among the quarters of fifteen or twenty different dates since the turn of the century that are worth far more than their original price. Still, there is a certain amount of historical interest in speculating on how these twenty-five-cent coins were spent in the years of their minting, for it was in 1951 that millions of people began investing their spare quarters in twenty-five-cent paperback books, which had just caught on like wildfire. In the middle of 1958, the first-class postage rate went up, so that someone who spent that 1958 quarter for postage in May or June could have sent five letters and five postcards with it, but after July first it would have been good for mailing only four letters and three postcards.

In short, what to some people might be only a dollar and seventeen cents' worth of change is to the coin collector an endless view into the colorful past and perhaps, with a little bit of foresight or luck, an occasional added bonus for a premium piece.

A very real problem for the novice collector is that of spreading himself too thin. There is an almost endless variety of coins, dating back more than twenty-six centuries—back to countries and peoples that no longer exist. Obviously, if you start collecting every kind of coin you can get hold of you soon will have a meaningless jumble, but if you stick to a few particular classes you should some day have a collection to be proud of.

The choice of classes is almost endless. For example, you can collect pennies, nickels, dimes, quarters, half-dollars, or silver dollars, trying to get either one of each type that has been minted or else a complete set of one type. A "type" is a coin's distinguishing design. Thus an Indian head is one type of cent and a Lincoln head is another.

Or you can try to secure specimens from all of the seven mints that have operated in the United States, or coins of colonial America or of some other country than the United States, or coins of ancient Greece or Rome, or coins from anywhere in the world having similar features in their design, such as ships, castles, animals, or trees.

Another idea is to collect a type set of U.S. coins issued in the year of your birth. Still another is to specialize in denominations that no longer are coined: half cents, two-cent pieces, silver and nickel three-centers, half dimes, twenty-cent pieces, and (if you can afford it) the various kinds of gold pieces.

Or you might try seeing how many versions of Liberty you can unearth. She has been pictured in an amazing number of ways: full length or just a head, slender or plump, wearing a cap, wearing a coronet, wearing a laurel wreath, seated or standing, letting her hair float loosely or having it arranged in a wide variety of styles.

Then there are the commemoratives—dozens of specially designed coins issued for brief periods in honor of famous persons or occasions in the American past. These form a fascinating field for history enthusiasts.

Some such enthusiasts, however, prefer picking their own fields of history: the Civil War period, for instance, or the California gold rush, or Presidential inauguration years. The possibilities are practically endless.

All but the wealthy should concentrate on coins of fairly recent years, for naturally those from earlier dates tend to be scarcer and more expensive, although age is not the only factor that gives coins premium value, and you still can buy some pieces minted more than a century ago for only a few times their original worth. Among the other factors are misstriking, overstriking, variations in dies, and scarcity caused not so much by age as by a small original issue.

A misstruck coin is precisely what its name suggests: one on which some little error was made in minting. One example of this was the 1800 half dime, where an engraver got a "K" mixed up with Liberty's "R," turning her into LIBEKTY. Naturally that misspelled Liberty is popular with collectors and commands a high price, just as do a number of other misstruck pieces.

An "overstrike" is a piece on which some feature of the inscription has been intentionally changed. In our mint's early days this was done fairly often; rather than cut a whole new die the engraver would simply put a new date over the old one, with results that are a delight to collectors, who will pay ten times as much for an 1800 half cent overstruck to read "1802" as they will for an 1800 coin that has not been altered. Even in fairly recent years there have been

6. *Overstruck 1800-02 half cent*

some instances of premium prices caused by overstriking; at the Denver Mint in 1918, for instance, an "8" was struck over what originally had been "7" in a number of '17 nickels.

Variations in dies are another cause for boosts in coin prices. Back in the days of hand-cut dies these variations happened frequently: when an engraver made a new die to replace a worn-out one he seldom could help allowing some slight change to creep into his work. Nowadays such changes no longer occur; dies still wear out, of course, but they are machine-made from the same master die, so all are exactly alike.

One of the commonest reasons for certain coins' high cash value is a simple one: only a small number were produced. Take, for example, $3 gold pieces, which have not been made since 1889. All of them have premium values, but the ones minted in 1875 sell for fifty or sixty times as much as those from 1874. Why? Because almost 42,000 such pieces were coined in '74, and only sixty (all proofs) the following year.

Such ups and downs as this in the number of coins turned out from year to year are frequent; the mint may strike anything from none at all to many millions, depending on current demand and the supply on hand. For this reason many a newcomer to collecting has been disappointed to learn that some piece which looks very rare, such as his cherished 1857 half dime, will not bring a high price if he tries to sell it. True, it may *look* rare, but the mints at Philadelphia and New Orleans struck over eight and a half million half dimes in 1857, so plenty of other collectors have its twin brothers. If this beginner's little coin had been minted eleven years earlier, however, its valuation would soar greatly, for only 27,000 half dimes were made in 1846.

And yet none of the reasons that have just been given—extreme age, misstriking, overstriking, variations in dies, and limited minting —quite explains one of the costliest of all American coins: the 1804 silver dollar. True, it is old, but the dollars coined from 1795 to

7. 1804 silver dollar

1803 are even older, yet they seldom are sold for excessively high sums, while the 1804 coins, on the rare occasions when they change hands, command prices of many thousand dollars.

Why? They were neither misstruck nor overstruck, and almost 20,000 of them were minted. Then why *are* they so scarce? No one seems to know for sure, but the best guess is that most of them were lost in some catastrophe such as a shipwreck, leaving only the twelve or fifteen for whose possession collectors have been competing ever since.

Novices have to be on their guard not to be hoodwinked by fakes of such rarities as this, for the altering of run-of-the-mill coins in order to make them look like more sought-after pieces is a common form of crime. The most frequent alteration to watch out for is the changing of a coin's date; this has been done, for example, with many of the numerous 1858 "flying eagle" cents to make them appear to be the uncommon 1856 flying eagles, of which only about a thousand were minted.

To avoid being taken in by such frauds is one of the reasons many coin enthusiasts not only belong to collectors' clubs, where advice and information can be exchanged, but also make a practice of consulting reliable coin dealers. Only the most ignorant beginner will let himself be taken in by the type of dealer who runs big, conspicuous ads suggesting that you can easily get thousands of dollars for old coins that you find lying around the house or receive in everyday change. It is far safer to do business with dealers who make no such extravagant promises.

As any dealer will tell you, a coin's condition is highly important. The most desirable and valuable coins are *proofs*. (Definitions of the various grades of condition listed here will be found, along with definitions of many other numismatic terms, in a special section at the back of this book.) Next in order come *uncirculated* pieces. Next come *extremely fine*, then *very fine*, then *fine*, then *very good*, then *good*, then *fair*, then *poor*, and, last of all, *mutilated*.

Except on very special occasions, the Philadelphia Mint is the only one that strikes proof coins. For many years it also was the only mint that did not identify its coins with a mint mark—a tiny letter showing where the coin was made. Until very recently every piece struck at Denver bore a D, and in years past there were also S for San Francisco, O for New Orleans, CC for Carson City (Nevada), C for Charlotte (North Carolina), and D for Dahlonega (Georgia). Having two separate "D's" is not as confusing as it sounds, for the branch mint at Dahlonega existed only from 1838 to 1861, while Denver's was not founded until 1906. When you have a pre-1966 coin without a mint mark, therefore, you can be almost sure that it came from Philadelphia.

Looking for mint marks soon becomes second nature to the collector, for one of those miniature letters may make a sizable difference in a coin's value. For example, a 1911 Denver quarter eagle ($2.50 gold piece) sells for seven or eight times as much as that same year's quarter eagle struck in Philadelphia. And all because of that little D!

A visit to a mint ranks high on every coin collector's list of sightseeing aims. And when you see those big machines stamping out coins by the thousands and millions you realize more than ever that Americans have come a long way from the time less than two centuries ago when the only coins they had were those made in other countries.

Chapter Two

POCKET-SIZE MONUMENTS

1492=1734

When Columbus came to the West Indies he probably brought with him some of the gold double *excelentes* that King Ferdinand and Queen Isabella had had minted to finance his explorations. Chances are, however, that he spent none of these coins in the New World, for the earliest visitors to the Atlantic's western shores had little use for money.

So it was with later explorers and colonists who followed Columbus. The Indians with whom they bargained were not interested in money; what they wanted were such things as nails, tools, cookpots, and cloth. Even when colonists traded with each other, they were more likely to barter than to use cash: a chicken might be swapped for two fish, a spare hat for spare gunpowder, and so forth. Tobacco, furs, cattle, and grain were all common substitutes for money.

8. Spanish double excelente of Ferdinand and Isabella

Most Indians preferred their own seashell money, wampum, to strange European coins, and before long many colonists began using wampum, too. Instead of coins they carried strings of polished dark and light shells, ground down to uniform size. These were commonly accepted almost everywhere; in 1640, in fact, the General Court of Massachusetts ruled that two pieces of blue wampum or fourteen pieces of white were legally equal to one English penny.

Making wampum a lawful form of money was probably more a matter of necessity than of trying to please the Indians. There simply were too few metal coins to meet the demand. The gold, silver, and copper pieces that trickled in from a dozen different European lands were not enough to fill the needs of traders who had to send hard cash back to Europe to pay for manufactured goods.

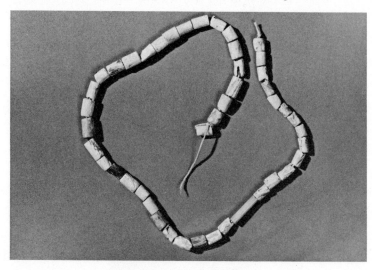

9. String of wampum

In the sixteenth century and the early part of the seventeenth there were no coins made in America except those struck by Spaniards in Mexico and Peru. You might think that England would have kept her colonists supplied with guineas, shillings, and pence, but England herself was so short on coins that she exported very few. (The coin shortage in Britain was due chiefly to the fact that for many years the metal in her silver coins was worth more than the face value of the coins themselves, so it was common practice for Englishmen to make a profit by melting down their money to be sold as silver.) To make the situation worse, English laws forbade colonists to coin money of their own. Therefore it is difficult to collect coins of the types used in America's early colonial years, for they were a mixture of sixteenth and seventeenth century pieces from Spain, England, Germany, Sweden, France, Holland, and other countries.

If we want coins to remind us of America's colonial period the best thing to do, probably, is to collect the commemorative half-dollars that our government has issued from time to time in honor of various events in our history. Not until 1892 did our first commemorative coin appear, celebrating Columbus's arrival in the New World four hundred years earlier. It was a silver half-dollar issued for what your great-grandfather called the "Chicago World's Fair," although its official name was "World's Columbian Exposition." On the Columbian half-dollar's face or obverse appears the discoverer's head, while on the reverse, spanning the earth's two hemispheres, is his jaunty flagship, the *Santa Maria*, with all sails billowing.

10. 1892 Columbian half-dollar

11. *1893 Isabella quarter*

12. *Old Spanish Trail half-dollar, 1935*

Because the big fair at Chicago ran for two years, 1893 brought not only a reissue of the Columbian half-dollar, but also a new and most unusual piece—the only quarter-dollar in the entire commemorative series. It features the crowned head of Columbus's patroness, Queen Isabella of Spain.

Thirty-six years after Columbus first landed in the West Indies, a Spaniard named Cabeza de Vaca, with a number of companions, set out across what is now Texas to seek a route to Mexico City. For nearly eight years nothing was heard of him. Then de Vaca and three others appeared in Mexico City with a tale of Indian captivity and hardship which had brought death to most of their party as they struggled along what has since come to be known as the Old Spanish Trail. Four hundred years later, in 1935, the United States honored the achievement of Cabeza de Vaca and his men by issuing the Old Spanish Trail half-dollar. The face of this piece shows the head of one of the longhorned cattle that the Spaniards introduced to the western world. On the coin's reverse is a map of the explorers' trail, together with one of those sword-leafed yucca trees that were such a familiar sight to them in their travels.

Probably the average American never has heard of Cabeza de Vaca, but most of us know at least a little about the "lost colony" that followers of Sir Walter Raleigh planted on Roanoke Island, off the coast of what is now North Carolina, half a century after the Spaniard's long trek. What happened to those brave British pioneers in the years between 1587 and 1591? All that anyone knows is that they and their little community had vanished when their leader returned to the New World after a four-year trip to England to round up supplies. Vanished along with them was Roanoke Island's prized baby, Virginia Dare, the first white child born to British colonists in this new land west of the ocean.

In 1937, 350 years later, the lost colony's memory was recalled by a half-dollar issued in its honor. On this commemorative's face is a bust of Sir Walter Raleigh, who actually never set foot in the colony, although he was the one who had planned this first tragic attempt to start a British settlement in America. On the coin's reverse is the famous but probably short-lived infant, Virginia Dare, held by her mother.

About twenty years after the lost colony's disappearance an English navigator, Henry Hudson, nosed his ship, the *Half Moon*, into a bay some four hundred miles north of Roanoke Island. He had been employed by the Dutch East India Company to seek the mythical Northwest Passage to India, in the search for which so many explorers risked their lives. Though he failed in his hope of finding that passage, he *did* find and explore the beautiful river that now bears his name. The memory of Hudson's journey up that river is recalled by a half-dollar sponsored in 1935 by the little city of Hudson, New York. On this coin's obverse is the good ship *Half Moon*, and on its reverse are some rather surprising figures drawn from ancient mythology; mounted on a whale is Poseidon, the Greek god of the sea whom the Romans called Neptune, with a finny-tailed mermaid disporting herself in the background.

13. Roanoke Island half-dollar, 1937

A decided contrast to Poseidon and his mermaid is found on the face of a commemorative honoring another notable ship that came to these shores eleven years after the *Half Moon's* 1609 voyage. That ship, of course, is the *Mayflower*, pictured on the half-dollar's reverse. The pious figure on its obverse, wearing Pilgrim garb, is William Bradford, long-time governor of the Pilgrims' Plymouth Colony in New England. This beautifully designed coin was issued in 1920, three centuries after the Pilgrims' landing on Plymouth Rock.

A third ship, the *New Netherland*, ornaments the reverse side of a commemorative that might have been quite different if Henry Hudson's search for the Northwest Passage had been sponsored by his native England instead of by the Dutch East India Company. Because the English Hudson was working for a Dutch firm, Holland naturally claimed ownership of the Hudson River region, and a year or so after the navigator's visit settlers from the Netherlands came to Manhattan Island to set up a trading post which they called New Netherland. In 1624 they were joined by a number of Protestants from Belgium and France known as Walloons and Huguenots.

In the three centuries that followed, the small trading post of New Netherland grew to be one of the largest cities in the world, and most of the millions of New Netherlanders (more commonly known as New Yorkers) had little or no idea of the part the Huguenots and the Walloons had played in their city's founding. But they were reminded of it in 1924 with the issuing of a new half-dollar inscribed HUGUENOT-WALLOON TERCENTENARY— FOUNDING OF NEW NETHERLAND. The heads on the coin's obverse (numismatists call overlapping heads like this "conjoined" or "jugate") are those of two Huguenot heroes who had been killed in European political strife years before New Netherland was dreamed of.

Another who, like these two Huguenots, never visited the New World, is the man whose head we see on the commemorative issued in 1934 to mark the 300th year of the first settlements made in Maryland. The head on Maryland's half-dollar is that of Cecil Calvert, the second Lord Baltimore, who inherited from his father a royal grant of land around that great arm of the Atlantic Ocean known as Chesapeake Bay. The second Lord Baltimore sent his brother, and later his son, to supervise his colony, but, though he lived for more than forty years after Maryland's founding, he preferred the comforts of his home in England to the hazards of a voyage across the ocean to see the land he had named for Queen Henrietta Maria, wife of his king, Charles I.

In that fourth decade of the seventeenth century new colonies and settlements were being established thick and fast. Not all of them (perhaps fortunately for coin collectors) have been the subject of commemorative coins, but in addition to Maryland there are five others which have received that distinction.

Connecticut, Rhode Island, and Delaware all had their first settlements within two years after Maryland's founding. The half-dollars marking these three colonies' tercentenaries feature important symbols of their early days. Connecticut's is the Charter Oak, a huge and beautiful tree in Hartford which had a convenient hollow in its trunk where the colonists are supposed to have hidden their precious charter when New England's British Governor-General demanded its surrender. Rhode Island's shows the colony's founder, Roger Williams, being welcomed by a friendly Indian on his arrival by canoe at the site of his "Providence Plantations." And Delaware's pictures not only the Swedish vessel *Kalmar Nyckel*, which brought the first permanent Swedish settlers to Fort Christina (later the city of Wilmington), but also the quaint "Old Swedes' Church," built during the settlement's early years.

Two other pioneering ventures in 1636 are recalled by commemorative half-dollars issued on their 300th anniversaries in 1936: the landing of Dutch settlers at Jamaica Bay on Long Island, and the founding of the first county (York) in the "Province of Maine."

Other events of the pre-Revolutionary period of which we are reminded by commemoratives are the granting of a city charter to Albany, New York, in 1686; the founding two years later of New Rochelle, New York, by Huguenots from La Rochelle, France; and the founding of Norfolk, Virginia, in 1736. (Albany, incidentally, was first settled seventy-two years before its city charter was granted.)

Except for the Columbian and the Old Spanish Trail half-dollars and the Queen Isabella quarter, all of the commemoratives we have examined so far have celebrated the beginnings of various colonies and settlements. The remaining coin connected with the colonial period is different, however: it is a half-dollar honoring the birth of Daniel Boone, the most famous of our frontiersmen, who blazed trails traveled by later pioneers. (The striking of this coin in Boone's memory came two centuries after he was born in Pennsylvania in 1734.)

Between 1892 and 1951 sixty different commemoratives were issued—fifty of silver and ten of gold. Of these only the seventeen having to do with events before the American Revolution have been described here. Like all others in this series, they are legal tender at their face value, but rarely can one of them be found in circulation. They hardly ever are spent like regular-issue coins, and any that show even slight signs of wear are seldom wanted by collectors. When they were issued, the groups sponsoring them usually bought them from the mint at their face value and then sold them as souvenirs at a higher price. Dealers and collectors were their chief purchasers, and most of those not sold within a reasonable time were returned to the mint for melting.

During the years recalled by those seventeen pre-Revolutionary commemoratives, our colonial ancestors were making use of a weird assortment of coins in their trading—an assortment so confusing as to make us grateful that today we have to deal only with cents, nickels, dimes, quarters, halves, and (rarely) silver dollars.

Chapter Three

COIN CONFUSION
IN THE COLONIES
1607-1775

Today you would never think of trying to pass off old medals as cash, but three or four hundred years ago if you had tried to use medals in place of money you probably would have met no objections. There were two reasons for this. First, money was so scarce in the non-Spanish part of America that anything looking at all like a coin was usually accepted. And, second, the available coins were so varied in design and origin that the average colonist could not know whether or not it was true when someone told him a guilder was as good as a florin or a crown was worth more than a thaler.

Amid all the mix-up of currency from a dozen different countries the one kind that almost everybody got to know and to trust in the North American colonies' early days were the pieces from Spain or from mints that the Spanish conquistadores had set up at Mexico City and Lima in the New World: cuartos, reales, pesos, excelentes, pistoles, and doubloons.

This is not surprising, for nearly all the highlights of sixteenth-century America had been Spanish: Ponce de Leon discovering Florida, Cortes reaching California, de Soto pushing westward to the Mississippi, Coronado introducing horses to the Southwest, Spaniards establishing at St. Augustine the first permanent white colony in what is now the United States. No wonder Spanish coins became the ones that people knew!

It is true that in 1498 John Cabot, sailing from England, discovered Newfoundland fifteen years before Ponce de Leon came to Florida, but he was so disappointed at not finding a passage to India that he did not linger, and if he and his men carried coins from England or from Cabot's native Italy they left none in the New World. This leads us to wonder whether the Vikings, who arrived in America almost five-hundred years before Columbus and Cabot, may have had Norse coins with them when they came to their "Vinland."

The first non-Spaniards from Europe who undoubtedly did make use of coins, as well as of barter and of wampum, were the pioneers from England who in 1607 settled Jamestown in Virginia. Both French and English settlements had been established along the coast of Maine before Jamestown was founded, but these colonies were too short-lived to engage in any real trade, whereas the Jamestown colonists sent cargoes of exports back to their mother country only a year after their arrival in America. During that first year of hard labor in the wilderness they somehow had found time to make soap and glass, and these they dispatched to England, along with by-products of the forests they had burned: pitch, tar, and precious wood ashes. After many months of waiting for their ship's return they welcomed it back from overseas loaded not only with the supplies they sorely needed but also with hard cash—the first cash income ever earned by Britain's American colonists.

James I was king at that time, so possibly his portrait appeared on the coins paying Jamestown's colonists for their goods. It is just as

14. British shilling, showing Henry VIII

likely, however, that the portraits were of Queen Elizabeth or Queen Mary or King Edward VI or Henry VIII or others who had ruled before James, for in those days coins were kept in service for a long span of years. They served, in fact, until they were worn so smooth that their inscriptions and devices could hardly be seen. Just how old their money was the people who used it seldom knew for sure, for only recently had the idea of putting dates on coins come into use, and some pieces still were undated. Their inscriptions generally were in Latin, and usually they were so much abbreviated that only an expert could understand them.

Chances are that the Jamestown settlers could not keep for long the money they received for their exports; they had to send their coins back to England to buy manufactured goods. But what else could they have done with them, anyway? The Indians with whom they traded preferred gay beads of glass to dingy metal disks, and in those early years there was no one except the Indians with whom to do business. Even when English girls were brought across the sea to be sold as wives it was not with money that the men paid for their brides, but with Virginia-grown tobacco—anywhere from a hundred to two hundred pounds of it.

Tobacco served instead of cash not only for buying wives, but also for buying slaves from the Dutch traders who brought to Virginia ships filled with Negroes captured in Africa. Sometimes, however, the Virginians paid for their slaves with English coins, instead of with tobacco, or the traders gave Dutch money for the tobacco they bought. That was the beginning of the continual mix-

up in coinage that was to plague the colonies up till and even after the Revolution.

The traders scurried back and forth along the coast in their little ships, for within thirty years after Jamestown's founding there were many other settlements: English in Virginia and Maryland and in many spots along the New England coast, Dutch and Swedish on the Hudson and Delaware Rivers, French in scattered colonies to the north and west. Henry Hudson and his followers had come, the Pilgrims had come, and in 1626 or thereabouts the Dutchman Peter Minuit had made his famous purchase of "Manhattes" Island from the Indians in exchange for cloth and other trade goods worth about sixty Dutch guilders or twenty-four Spanish pieces of eight. And the traders, visiting first one colony and then another, often had no choice but to accept English shillings or French écus or Swedish kroner for their wares, when what they really wanted were the guilders and stuyvers of their own Netherlands.

There was another kind of currency, too, that appeared sometimes in the early colonial days. It was popularly called "hogge money" because of the picture of a pig on its obverse, and the traders picked it up on their way across the ocean when they stopped to do business at the Somers Islands (now known as Bermuda). These brass shillings, sixpence, threepence, and twopence, issued from 1616 to 1624, were the first coins ever made solely for the use of England's colonies overseas. They featured hogs because the first British mariners to visit these bits of land far off the Carolina coast had left

15. Somers Island "hogge money"

a few pigs, and these animals, running wild, had increased so greatly in number that they caused the islands to be nicknamed "the Hogge Islands."

By this time the Jamestown colonists were not the only ones shipping cargoes to Europe. Massachusetts Bay, Plymouth, and New Netherland settlers were also receiving the money of their homelands in payment for such New World goods as lumber and furs. And, as the settlements flourished, the need increased for coins from overseas. The Massachusetts Bay colonists, for instance, could use cattle, furs, and farm products to pay their taxes, but if they wanted to ride across the Charles River on the ferry between the new, fast-growing towns of Charlestown and Boston, they had to pay a penny apiece for their fares. (The massive English penny, of course, was worth twice as much as the later American cent.)

With new enterprises constantly springing up, colonists needed money for many other purposes, as well. For one thing, there were taverns now where meals could be bought, although in the Massachusetts seaport town of Salem the lawgivers tried in 1633 to prevent innkeepers from profiteering by laying down the rule that not more than sixpence could be charged for any meal. And money was needed for the double ruffles and silk shoe rosettes than men wore when they were dressed in their best, and for sending mail at one penny per letter through the first post office in the colonies, established in Massachusetts in 1639.

Most amazing of all, in a land which a few years before had been wilderness, money was needed for buying "made-in-America" books, for in 1636 the first printing press in the colonies was set up in the Massachusetts town of Cambridge, and there, four years later, was published the famous *Bay Psalm Book*. The Puritan Fathers who grudgingly spent a few shillings for their copies of this hymnal would doubtless have been astounded to know that three centuries later a book collector would pay $151,000 for one of the few surviving specimens of that first American book.

16. *New England shilling,*
1652

Continual shortage of cash to pay for these new goods and services made the citizens of Massachusetts feel more and more discontented with their lack of coinage. When repeated appeals to their British overlords brought no results, they took the matter into their own hands, defying the English colonial law against producing money in the colonies. Though the men of Massachusetts were law-abiding in most ways, they could not see why the making of coins meant only for New England was going to do old England any harm, so in 1652 they set up their own mint.

From that pioneer mint in Boston there came for nearly thirty-five years some of the most famous coins ever struck in America. At first they were simple disks of silver, quite bare except for the initials NE on one side and the Roman numerals XII or VI or III on the other. The NE stood for New England and the Roman numerals meant twelvepence (one shilling), sixpence, and threepence. But their plainness turned out to be a serious fault, for it was all too easy to counterfeit them or to trim silver from their unmarked edges.

After a few months, therefore, the NE coins were replaced by pieces ornamented with trees: first a willow, then an oak, then a

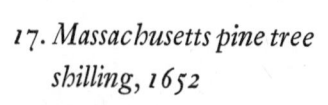

17. *Massachusetts pine tree*
shilling, 1652

pine. Each coin also bore on its obverse the words MASATHU-SETS IN, and on the reverse NEW ENGLAND, AN DOM (for anno Domini) 1652, with a Roman numeral showing value.

A curious thing is that, although these "tree" coins continued to be made until 1687, all but a few of them bore 1652 as their date. The idea behind this back-dating seems to have been that it would fool British authorities into thinking that Massachusetts no longer was making its own coins, but it hardly seems likely the British were that easily fooled.

When travelers went from Massachusetts to one of the other colonies they often had to exchange their Boston-minted coins for other kinds, just as travelers have to do in Europe today when they travel between countries. Because of this problem our ancestors had to draw up complicated schedules showing how much one kind of coinage was worth in terms of another. This was a frequent cause for quarrels, for it sometimes seemed that no two colonies could agree even on how much English and Spanish coins were worth, let alone such upstart issues as New England's.

Six years after Massachusetts started minting coins, Maryland, too, began having its own brand of money: copper pennies and silver shillings, sixpence, and fourpence. These were all minted in London in 1658 by order of Lord Baltimore whose bust appeared 276 years later on Maryland's commemorative half-dollar. His profile and the Latin form of his name (CAECELIUS) are on the 1658 coins' faces, along with TERRAE MARIAE (land of Mary). On the reverse is a Latin inscription meaning, in English, "Increase and multiply." (To acquire a much larger population was one of the main aims of all the colonies.) Maryland's scarce copper pennies,

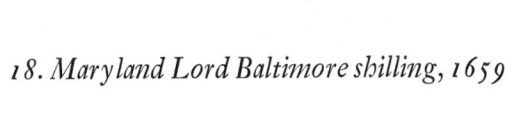

18. Maryland Lord Baltimore shilling, 1659

incidentally, bring far higher prices in today's collectors' markets than do its silver coins of much greater original face value.

Unlike New England and Maryland, the colony of New Netherland made no money of its own. Its coinage was in a lively state of confusion after this Dutch stronghold was taken over by the British in 1664. The new proprietorship meant, among other things, that people who always had thought of money in terms of guilders and stuyvers were now supposed to deal with crowns, shillings, and pence. As a matter of fact, however, there was not nearly enough British money to go around, so when New Netherland became New York the night watchmen who had been keeping order in the town for a wage of twenty-four stuyvers (about two shillings) a night probably continued to receive their pay in stuyvers instead of shillings.

In 1673 the colonists in New England and in the newly English territory along the Hudson took a revolutionary step: they established a scheduled mail service between Boston and New York, with mail carriers on fast horses riding at regular intervals along what came to be known as the Boston Post Road. There were no postage stamps yet, of course; persons to whom mail was addressed were charged a fee before they could receive their letters, although sometimes senders paid postage in advance. To cover these postal fees the colonists offered a wide variety of coins, not only New England's, Britain's, Holland's, and Spain's, but also coins from France that were commonly used in the many French settlements in Maine and in what is now Canada.

These French pieces, known as sols and deniers, were minted in 1670 and 1672 especially for France's colonies overseas. Quite possibly Louis Joliet and Father Marquette carried some with them in 1673 and 1674 when they made their explorations of the upper Mississippi and set up their mission on the site where Chicago now stands.

A few years later the Province of New Jersey also had some

special coins of its own—halfpennies and farthings that had been brought over from Ireland by a money-minded colonist named Mark Newby, who persuaded the Jersey Province's General Assembly to give its official approval to use of his coins. Truly unusual they were, too, for the likeness they bore was that of St. Patrick driving the snakes out of Ireland, and the legend on the halfpenny was (in Latin) "May the King prosper!", while that on the farthing was "May the people be quiet!"

It was in 1682, the same year that the last of these St. Patrick coins began to circulate in New Jersey, that across the Delaware River (where the Swedes had had settlements since the 1640's) William Penn and the Quakers founded their city of Philadelphia and province of Pennsylvania. In short order this latecomer among the colonies became one of the most flourishing of them all, with settlers pouring in not only from England and Wales but also from other parts of Europe, particularly Germany.

You might think that fast-growing Pennsylvania would have been one of the colonies to have coinage of its own, but it never did, perhaps because William Penn disapproved strongly of the New World's complicated mixture of money. He continually urged the adoption of one standard coinage throughout the colonies, but nearly a century had to pass before this dream of Penn's was finally realized.

Meanwhile the local coinages continued to multiply. There were the lion-decorated copper tokens made in London for New England in 1675 and the 1688 pewter "plantation tokens" featuring a horse

19. New Jersey's St. Patrick farthing

and armored rider that were widely used in the southern colonies. There were the GOD PRESERVE CAROLINA AND THE LORDS PROPRIETORS and GOD PRESERVE NEW ENG-LAND copper halfpennies of 1694, each displaying a large elephant. There was the brass spread-eagle token issued in Holland in 1700 for (according to the inscription) NEW YORKE IN AMERICA. There were the brass "Virginia shillings" or "Gloucester tokens" of 1714; and in Massachusetts, Pennsylvania, and South Carolina there was even money made of paper.

In none of this currency did the colonists have as much faith, however, as they had in the Spanish piastre, commonly called peso or piece of eight because it was worth eight reales. Now *there*, they felt, was real money you could count on not to lose its value! And around the turn of the century they busied themselves with picks and shovels, trying to increase their stock of these famous coins, for they had heard rumors that a pirate named Captain Kidd had been burying his ill-gotten wealth on various beaches all the way up and down the Atlantic coast, as well as on a scattered assortment of islands. From mouth to mouth and from settlement to settlement there spread stories, ever increasing in grandeur, of those hidden chests full of Spanish doubloons, pistoles, and pieces of eight that Captain Kidd had captured on the Spanish Main. Digging in the sand became a favorite pastime which continued even after the dreaded pirate was hanged for his crimes in 1701, for Kidd went to his death without ever revealing his treasure's whereabouts.

20. Seventeenth century Spanish "piece of eight"

Among the new things on which to spend money around this time was tea, a pleasant beverage from the East Indies which recently had been introduced in the colonies. In the bigger towns there were a few newspapers, too, and in Virginia's capital town of Williamsburg there was even a theater, built in 1716. Also there were books, the most widely sold of which were *The Pilgrim's Progress* for grown-ups and *Mother Goose's Melodies for Children*.

One of those who read every newspaper and book he could lay his hands on was a runaway printer's apprentice from Boston named Benjamin Franklin, who made his way down the coast to Philadelphia by way of New York in 1723, arriving in the Quaker City with what he later described in his *Autobiography* as "a Dutch dollar"—all that was left of the money he had raised for his journey by selling some of his books. A Dutch dollar went a long way in Philadelphia in 1723; with it Franklin bought not only loaves of bread he ate as he wandered through the streets, but also his midday dinner, his supper, and a night's lodging in an inn. Even after all this outlay he still had some money left, which is not surprising, when you consider that a dollar was four or five times as much as a laborer could earn in a day.

What *was* Franklin's "Dutch dollar"? It might have been a rixdollar from Holland, which was worth two and a half guilders or just about as much as a piece of eight. More probably, however, it was one of the silver reichstalers from Germany that were then in common use in Pennsylvania.

Even so agile a mind as Ben Franklin's must have been sorely puzzled sometimes as to just how much his money was worth, if we can judge by a letter that another newcomer to Philadelphia, John Christopher Sauer, wrote to friends in Germany in 1724. "Whoever brings gold pistoles," Sauer told them, "earns half a reichstaler on each florin. One loses with ducats. Whoever exchanges for English crowns in England and receives for them copper money in England profits one hundred with one hundred . . . Gold coins and ducats are cut so small that one can buy a pound of butter with a small piece. They are not readily accepted, however, for paper money is preferred."

That was one of the surprising things young Franklin was to learn in Philadelphia. In Boston, his native city, paper money was used a little, but most people distrusted it. But "In Pennsylvania" (as another German immigrant wrote home a few years later) "everything is paid for with stamped paper money . . . This . . . is printed in English and bears the King's seal and the governor's name." This paper currency, he said, was to be had in ten different denominations, ranging from twopence to a pound, "or" (as he explained) "in German money six florins. Such a piece of paper money . . . no bigger than a hand's breadth . . . may be exchanged for silver and gold. Anyone who counterfeits such officially stamped paper money is hanged without any possibility of pardon."

Throughout the colonies, in addition to the many kinds of coins mentioned before, there were a number of others which served to keep Americans in a state of financial confusion. One series, the "Rosa Americana" halfpennies, pennies, and twopence, were issued in England in 1722–23 (and a few in 1724 and 1733 and as late as 1760), solely for use in America. They drew their name from the rose on their reverse, beneath the royal crown. It is the legend on the obverse, however, that arouses curiosity. When translated from its Latin abbreviations, it says: "George, by the grace of God king of Great Britain, of France, and of Ireland." That is a truly surprising statement, for the King of France at that time was Louis XV,

21. Rosa Americana penny, 1722

and the hard-to-explain claim made for George I in the coin's inscription shows once again what a busy role coins play in recording history, even though this history sometimes may be a bit twisted to suit the whims of rulers.

The Rosa Americanas met with a chilly reception on this side of the Atlantic because they were so light in weight. Their manufacturer had figured that he could earn a bigger profit if he made them of a light alloy called Bath metal, but the colonists were as suspicious of them as you are today when you are given coins that seem to be too light in weight. What they wanted were heavy coins like the ones they were used to, not newfangled things that did not feel like money.

Along with his Rosa Americana this same economical manufacturer (an Englishman named William Wood) shipped across the ocean a lot of George I copper halfpennies and farthings featuring on the reverse a lady with a harp and the inscription HIBERNIA. Since neither harps nor the name "Hibernia" were commonly associated with the colonies this seems a bit puzzling until you learn that Mr. Wood originally had made the coins for Ireland, under authority granted him by King George I. He had made the error however, of failing to consult the Irish Privy Council about the design, and when the council's members saw the coppers they refused to accept them. Yet Mr. Wood was not stuck with a batch of unusable coins, for the British authorities apparently figured, correctly, that in America almost anything would pass.

22. Wood's Hibernia halfpenny, 1722

Around this time the continuing need for small change gave a Connecticut business man the idea of producing some copper coins of his own. John Higley of Granby had a copper mine and a furnace for refining his ore, and in 1737 he converted part of that furnace into his own private mint, striking there the first copper money ever made in America. They were attractive little pieces, bearing on the face a deer and the words THE VALUE OF THREE PENCE, while the inscription on the reverse proclaimed CONNECTICUT. 1737. Before long, however, Higley must have realized that these inscriptions might get him in trouble with the British authorities, so although he kept the deer he changed everything else, omitting the date and the CONNECTICUT and altering the VALUE OF THREE PENCE legend to VALUE ME AS YOU PLEASE.

From a modern point of view those privately minted Higley tokens and some of the other informal coins that appeared from time to time are truly puzzling. They seem to have been issued mainly by businessmen to overcome the lack of small change, but how did they get into circulation? Who decided how much they were worth? What was to prevent everyone from striking such coins to fill his own needs at any time? And, with so many different kinds of money circulating, how was the ordinary man to tell the counterfeit from the real? In short, the confusion of colonial currency was increasing all the time.

It was in the 1760's that the name George III began to appear on coins minted in England. Many colonists viewed the king's likeness with distaste, for they were feeling extremely bitter about the British Parliament's action in making them pay taxes to England whenever

23. Virginia's George III halfpenny, 1772

they imported tea, glass, lead, oil, paper, and various other things that they needed. Resenting these taxes, numerous Americans stopped buying items on which they had to pay import duties. After enduring this loss of trade for a while, England repealed the hated Stamp Acts—repealed all of them, that is, except the tax on tea.

Curious mementos of the Stamp Act repeal are the copper half-pennies and farthings known as "Pitt tokens," issued in Philadelphia in 1766. On the face, encircled by the legend THE RESTORER OF COMMERCE. NO STAMPS, they bear the likeness of big-nosed William Pitt, who had led the opposition in Parliament to taxation of American colonists. And on the reverse, surrounding a full-rigged ship bound for America, are the words THANKS TO THE FRIENDS OF LIBERTY AND TRADE. Here is a coin that records history as clearly as does a newspaper!

For a little while the Americans' anger died down, and anyone looking at the halfpennies, pennies, and shillings made in England for Virginia in 1773 and '74 would never guess that the colonists had any plans other than to remain England's loyal subjects indefinitely, for these Virginia coins, with their George III name and portrait and their crown-capped British seal, are particularly royalist in their design. But, unfortunately for the British, the year 1773 was marked not only by the issue of Virginia's special coinage but also by the enactment of new taxes on tea that roused Americans to fury.

What happened then is such common knowledge as to need no repeating. Not much more than a year after the Boston Tea Party a Virginian who probably had some of George III's Virginia coins in his pocket was crying "Give me liberty or give me death!" And with the Revolution which followed close upon that cry there came a time of such complications in the realm of money as to make the colonial period's mixed-up coinage seem almost simple by comparison!

Chapter Four

IN THE NEW
UNITED STATES
1775-1792

If the thirteen colonies had taken as long in uniting to fight for independence as they did in getting together on coinage, our history books might have an entirely different story to tell. From the time of the Revolution's first battles in 1775 to the opening of the U.S. Mint in 1792, several dozen different kinds of money were used in the new United States, and even so there was a constant shortage of hard cash.

So severe was this shortage at the Revolution's beginning that in 1775 the Continental Congress arranged to print two million dollars' worth of paper currency. As time went on the amount of paper money was increased to more than a hundred times that much. Meanwhile, however, its value went down and down until the Congress's original promise to redeem its currency in Spanish silver dollars, plus interest, became a bitter mockery. What was supposed to be a hundred dollars' worth of paper bills would not bring in exchange a single dollar's worth of silver or copper.

Because of the familiar and scornful expression, "not worth a Continental," referring to those almost worthless bills, many people have the mistaken idea that paper currency was the only kind of money issued by the Continental Congress. Actually Congress also authorized some metal coins—coins which, unlike the ill-fated paper, are of considerable value today.

The first of these, the huge pieces known as "Continental dollars," were struck in 1776. Nobody seems to know for sure whether they were minted in Philadelphia, in London, or in Lancaster, Pennsylvania, where the Congress fled for a brief time when British troops threatened Philadelphia. Some of them are made of pewter and some of brass, while the rarest and most valuable are of silver. On their face, in addition to CONTINENTAL CURRENCY and the date, they feature the sun and a sundial, with the words FUGIO (Latin for "I fly") and MIND YOUR BUSINESS—meaning, apparently, that time flies and therefore should not be wasted. On the reverse is a circular chain of thirteen rings, each bearing the name of a state, and in the middle of this circle is the proud statement WE ARE ONE, surrounded by AMERICAN CONGRESS. Certainly that is a coin with a tale to tell!

For eleven years after these dollars appeared there were no other coins representing all the colonies, but then in 1787 the Congress ar-

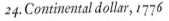

24. Continental dollar, 1776

ranged for the issue of three-hundred tons of copper cents similar in design to Continental dollars. Unlike the dollars, however, they take their popular name from their Latin motto and are generally known as "Fugio cents."

Eleven years is a long stretch, and Continental dollars were never numerous in the first place, so with paper currency of such little value, Americans of that era would have been hard pressed for something to use as money if it had not been for coins from various other sources. Of these there were so many as to make it seem as if almost everybody must have been striking coinage.

Most of these pieces were made in the 1780's, after the war was over, although Massachusetts produced cents and halfpennies in 1776 and Rhode Island had copper tokens in '78 and '79. In 1776 New Hampshire, too, made patterns for copper cents, but none of these ever were struck for general use. Later, in spite of the Continental Congress's 1785 ruling that states must not coin money, several other states and even some cities joined the procession: Connecticut from '85 to '88, New York in '86 and '87, New Jersey from '86 to '88, Massachusetts again in '87 and '88, Annapolis in '83, and Baltimore in '90.

Meanwhile dozens of new types of coins poured in from overseas —mainly from England, where businessmen, apparently bearing no grudge against the victorious colonists, were eager to secure contracts to supply the new country's coinage. Even before Cornwallis surrendered at Yorktown there were "North American tokens,"

25. Fugio cent, 1787

which arrived from abroad in 1781. After them came "Georgius Triumpho" cents in '83; "Nova Constellatio" cents in '83, '85, and '86; "Bar," "Confederatio," and "Immune Columbia" cents in '85; "Auctori Plebis" cents in '87; and "Mott tokens" in '89.

There were, moreover, at least twenty types of cents, half-dollars, and halfpennies featuring likenesses of George Washington, beginning in 1783 and continuing until even after the mint was opened in 1792. Out of this score of Washington designs only one— the half-dollar of 1792—was made in America; all the rest came from that same England against which Washington had been leading his infant nation's armies!

26. *Washington half-dollar, 1792*

Although the great majority of these post-Revolutionary coins were cents, there is one big exception: the Brasher doubloon, designed and issued privately in 1787 by Ephraim Brasher, a New York goldsmith. An imitation of the famous Spanish doubloon, this piece had a face value of $16, which was then a fairly vast sum of money. Probably it was used only by well-to-do businessmen in commercial dealings. Today it is so rarely found that it is worth thousands of dollars.

27. *1787 Brasher doubloon*

Also in circulation, in addition to the usual Spanish and English pieces, were Hesse thalers and other German money, brought to this country by the German soldiers whom the British had hired to fight for them. The American rebels, furious at the German mercenaries whose only interest in the war was the money they could make out of it, took to calling these coins "blood money."

Counterfeits were plentiful, of course, for with so many different kinds of coins around there were few people who could be certain what was genuine and what was not. So bad did the situation get that in the last few years before the United States started to make its own money more than half of the copper coins in circulation were counterfeits.

Whether their coins were counterfeit or genuine, foreign-made or American-made, people found as always, numerous ways of spending them. First of all, naturally, money had to go for daily necessities—necessities so expensive in wartime that often no cash was left for anything else. Still, even with times at their hardest, certain other things somehow managed to sell briskly. Early in 1776, for instance, there was Thomas Paine's stirring little book, *Common Sense*, urging the colonies to cut their ties with Britain. With whatever coins they happened to possess, people rushed to buy this; a hundred thousand copies were sold in less than three months.

A few months later another best seller was published. It was the July 6 issue of the *Pennsylvania Evening Post*, a three-times-a-week newspaper costing "two coppers." The *Post*, a modest, four-page journal, normally did not attract too much attention. What caused so many persons to pay out their two coppers for it on July 6, 1776, was that its whole first page and part of its second were given over to printing the full text of a thrilling document that the Continental Congress had passed two days before: the Declaration of Independence.

After another year or so those patriots who could afford it were saving their coins in order to buy the new flags of thirteen stars and thirteen stripes that the Congress had adopted for the United States. By that time, however, coins had nearly disappeared from circulation. Not till 1783, when the long war was over, did the average American have either any money to spend or anything available to buy. That was the year when Noah Webster published his famous *Speller*, and when it was also possible to purchase the first English Bible ever issued in America, produced in Philadelphia the year before. Either one or the other of these books, bought with the mixed-up coins of the period, found its way into the home of almost every American who knew how to read.

Soon there began to be all kinds of interesting things on which to spend money, if you happened to have it: theatrical performances, magazines, silver pump buckles, dictionaries, and fine dinnerware from Canton, China. If you wanted to travel you could buy a seat on one of the stagecoaches that in 1785 began to run regularly between Philadelphia, New York, Albany, and Boston, but for such trips you needed to have far more cash with you than was required for your fare, for to go the full distance took almost nine days, and most passengers had to pay for food and lodging at taverns along the way.

Even more novel than the stagecoach lines were the new boats powered by steam that in 1787 began to carry fare-paying passengers on the Delaware River between Philadelphia and Burlington. To enjoy such pleasures as this required more money than the average workman and his family possessed, and in 1786, mindful of the Declaration of Independence's ringing statement that "all men are created equal," the printers of Philadelphia went on strike for more pay. They won their strike, too, and as a result began to earn the princely wage of six dollars a week. The dollars they received were probably the highly favored Spanish piastres or pieces of eight, for it is doubtful if there were enough of the 1776 Continental dollars in circulation to meet the weekly payrolls.

By that time almost everybody had begun to complain about the lack of American coinage, and in 1785 Thomas Jefferson proposed to the Continental Congress that the United States set up its own coinage system. The unit of value, he said, should be a silver dollar equal to the well-loved Spanish eight-reale piece, but drawing its name from that of the German thaler. He also suggested a silver coin for a tenth of a dollar, a copper one for a hundredth, and a gold piece for ten dollars. He was particularly anxious, for the sake of what he called "easy arithmetic," that our coinage should be based on the decimal system, instead of on a confusing array of pounds, sovereigns, guineas, crowns, shillings, and pence, such as England had.

Most of the Congressmen agreed with him on this; as patriots of the new nation that had just broken away from subjection to the British king they had no desire to include any "sovereigns" or "crowns" in their coinage, and they felt that the Spanish system was far more practical. Before putting Jefferson's plan into effect, however, they argued about it for a long while. There were still many problems to be ironed out, such as how heavy the dollar should be (the Spanish one had varied in weight) and what kind of agreement could be made between the states on the worth of various coins.

It was not until August of 1786 that Congress adopted a coinage plan providing for a $5 gold piece, a silver dollar, silver coins worth 1/2, 1/4, 1/10, and 1/20 of a dollar, and copper coins worth 1/100 and 1/200 of a dollar. After six years of delay the mint was built at Philadelphia, in 1792, to put this plan into action.

Yet even though the mint did not open for business until sixteen years after the Declaration of Independence was signed and three years after Washington's inauguration as President, we have in our official U.S. coinage a number of pieces to remind us of that critical period in American history. These reminders are all part of our commemorative series.

First of the events thus noted is the Battle of Lexington and Concord in 1775. The Lexington-Concord half-dollar was issued

28. 1925 Lexington-Concord commemorative
half-dollar

in 1925 on the 150th anniversary of that April day when, according to Emerson, "the embattled farmers stood, and fired the shot heard round the world." On this silver coin's face appears one of the minutemen who seized muskets to protest against what they called the "intolerable acts" of their British overlords.

One of the most memorable of all dates in American history, the signing of the Declaration of Independence in Philadelphia in 1776, is brought to mind by two special coins struck a century and a half later: a $2.50 gold piece and a silver half-dollar. The former has on its face a standing figure of Liberty and on its reverse Philadelphia's Independence Hall. The silver piece features on its reverse Independence Hall's most famous relic, the Liberty Bell, and on its obverse the conjoined heads of George Washington and Calvin Coolidge, who was President in 1926.

One colony which did *not* sign the Declaration was Vermont. This was largely because New York and New Hampshire had long been squabbling as to which of them owned the territory that we now know as Vermont, and New York refused to allow the Green Mountain region to become a separate colony. With the Revolution's

29. 1926 U.S. Independence commemorative
half-dollar

outbreak, however, Vermonters joined the other colonists in fighting, and in 1777 they not only triumphed in the Battle of Bennington but also announced firmly that they were setting up an independent state owing no more allegiance to New York and New Hampshire than it did to the King of England.

A century and a half later, in 1927, the mint struck a silver half-dollar commemorating these two great moments in Vermont history. On the coin's face is the head of Ira Allen, who, with his brother Ethan and the famed "Green Mountain Boys," led Vermont to independence and military glory. On the reverse is one of the mountain lions whom the Green Mountain Boys were supposed to resemble in their fighting methods.

The same year that brought Vermont into the limelight brought to the fledgling United States a youthful French nobleman who was filled with admiration for George Washington and the Colonies' battle for liberty. So important a part did the young Marquis de Lafayette play in the Colonies' victory that in the 1890's American school children began raising money for a memorial to express their gratitude to him. The nickels and dimes they contributed built a statue in Paris. In 1900, when this statue was dedicated, the mint struck a "Lafayette dollar" of silver, showing on its face the heads of Washington and Lafayette and on its reverse a replica of the

30. 1900 Lafayette commemorative dollar

statue itself, portraying the young Frenchman mounted on horse-back. Among all our commemoratives this is the only silver dollar.

The year after Lafayette arrived in America the fabulous British mariner, Captain James Cook, came by accident upon those delightful bits of land in the Pacific Ocean that he dubbed the Sandwich Islands, which is what many people called Hawaii even in our great-grandfathers' day. A commemorative half-dollar minted 150 years later recalls this discovery, showing Captain Cook on its face and a native Hawaiian chief on its reverse. When it appeared in 1928 Hawaii had not yet become a state.

Two other half-dollars have their roots in this period between the Revolution's outbreak and the mint's opening. Both were sponsored by southern cities: Columbia, South Carolina, and Lynchburg, Virginia. The former marks the 150th anniversary of Columbia's becoming the state capital in 1786, and the latter the anniversary of Lynchburg's founding in that same year.

These, like all commemoratives, are of interest chiefly to coin collectors, who probably were an unknown breed in this country in the years just after the Revolution. At that time, all that the average American could hope for in the way of coinage was that his new government would soon be able to supply him with enough official, standardized cash for everyday use to take the place of the crazy mixture of currency that was so confusing to everybody. People thought that with the coming of the Federal Mint their headaches about coinage would be over, but soon they were to find that their problems were not that easily solved.

Chapter Five

THE MINT'S FIRST YEARS
1792=1812

George Washington's household account book tells us that on May 25, 1793, he spent $1.60 for "hire of a washerwoman 4 days," and two weeks later $9.00 for "4 pairs silk stockings for the President." Just what kind of coins were used for these payments we cannot know for sure, but certainly they were not produced at the new U.S. Mint in Philadelphia, for by June of 1793 the only pieces it had turned out were some cents and half cents and perhaps a few half "dismes" (which is how "dimes" was then spelled).

The mint had a hard time getting really started. The need for it was considered so pressing that one of the Federal Government's very first acts was to erect a mint building. But far more than a building was needed before coins could be made. First there had to be metal, and that was not easy to come by. Everyone was invited to turn in gold, silver, and copper to be transformed into coins at no charge, but people were slow to respond.

Legend says that George Washington started things going by letting the mint melt some of his silverware to make the 1792 half dismes. The first metal actually purchased for coinage was six pounds of old copper nails and scrap in 1793. Not until 1794 was there enough silver on hand to be of any real use. In July of that year the Bank of Maryland deposited in the mint over $80,000 worth of French coins to be melted and made into American money. With this solid nest egg the mint was able to go into real action at last.

The designing of the first U.S. coins seemed so important that almost every senator and representative wanted to have a hand in it. Congress held lengthy debates on the subject, and great numbers of trial patterns were prepared. Finally, an Act of Congress laid down strict rules for the mint's designers to follow.

As required by these rules, all coins—gold, silver, and copper—bore on their faces the date, the word LIBERTY, and the head of that ancient Roman Goddess of Liberty whom our American

31. First coining press used in the U.S. Mint

ancestors adopted as their own patroness. The gold and silver pieces also featured an array of stars—one for each state in the Union. The original idea was to add a new star each time a new state was added, just as is done with the flag, but soon states began coming in so rapidly that this plan was dropped.

On the reverse side, according to Congress's orders, all gold and silver coins had to show an eagle and the inscription UNITED STATES OF AMERICA. (After much debate, the eagle, standing for freedom, had been decided upon as our national bird, although a number of congressmen had favored the turkey.) Curiously enough, the coins bore no words or figures on either obverse or reverse to indicate how much they were worth. Some had raised letters around their outer rims to tell their value, but after these wore off, as they soon did, you had to judge merely from a coin's size whether it was a dollar, half-dollar, quarter, dime, or half dime.

The copper pieces had no eagle on the back, but within their circular UNITED STATES OF AMERICA inscription were the words ONE CENT or HALF CENT, surrounded by a wreath. They also had the figures 1/100 and 1/200, so that there could be no doubt as to exactly what their relationship was to the dollar. Oddly enough, although they were struck by the U.S. Mint, they were not legal tender in the United States until 1864; this means that anyone who wanted to be stubborn could legally refuse to receive copper coins in payment of debt.

Another thing worth noting is that none of the currency bore likenesses of George Washington, although dozens of unofficial portrait coins honoring him had been in circulation for years. Indeed, seven or eight additional types of Washington coins, all unofficial, appeared as late as 1795, which must have been confusing to citizens who were trying to get used to their government's own new coinage. So accustomed were people in that era to portraits of kings on their money that many of them felt our President's head should appear there, just as royalty's had done. But Washington himself would have none of this idea; having fought for freedom from royalty, he did not want to see his new nation exalting any living ruler on its coinage. Some authorities believe, however, that the woman's head on our early dimes is a portrait of Martha Washington.

Even after metal had been secured and coin designs had been decided upon, the mint still worked slowly, for of course every step in the coin-making process took far longer then than it does today. A modern machine can turn out as many coins in a minute or so as a man could make in a week when the mint was new. In those days each coin had to be milled separately in a hand-turned screw press, and production was far too slow to meet the demand.

Moreover, the engravers had to cut new dies when old ones wore out, and even though they tried to copy their models faithfully they could hardly help making occasional changes and errors. Therefore the coins of early America appear in a wide variety that causes today's uniform, machine-made pieces to seem rather dull by comparison. You will find STATES imprinted over STETES, LIBERTY misspelled LIHERTY, 1/200 with a clumsy "1" stamped over the "2" to make it read 1/100, "1802" struck over "1800," "1811" struck over "1809," and various other errors and corrections.

To the coin collector such wide variation is exciting, but far less pleasant is the matter of the frequent forgery of scarce early pieces. Anyone purchasing coins of this period should have an expert's advice to make sure he is not being deceived.

There is some difference of opinion as to which coins were the first ones made at the mint. According to mint records they were the cents and half cents of 1793, yet some dismes, half dismes, and cents of official U.S. design appeared in 1792—the same year that the newly organized U.S. Post Office began carrying letters as far as 30 miles for six cents, from 30 to 60 miles for eight cents, and from 60 to 150 miles for ten cents. Probably those 1792 coins were fashioned by mint employees working in temporary quarters until the permanent building was ready. They are, naturally, very scarce and expensive pieces. Perhaps the most interesting of all is the small 1792 cent that has a silver plug in its center. Its diameter of less than an inch is of as much interest as its silver plug, for, except for this one experiment, all cents made until 1857 measured about 1-1/8 inch, as contrasted with our present cent, which is only 3/4 inch across.

Even the half-cent pieces of those days were larger than modern cents. You might think that Americans of the 1790's and early 1800's, being accustomed to English halfpennies, would have taken half cents for granted, but for some unknown reason they disliked them and often refused to accept them, just as some persons of our own time refuse to accept $2 bills. Therefore, half cents always were minted in fairly small quantities, which explains why today they frequently are more expensive than all but the rarer types of large cents.

Working as fast as it could with its slow equipment, the mint issued its first silver coins in 1794. Only dollars, half-dollars, and half dimes were struck in that year, however. The first dimes and quarters were minted in 1796, and after that there were no more quarters until 1804.

The next year, 1795, brought the first appearance on U.S. coinage of words that we now find on all our coins and some of our paper money: E PLURIBUS UNUM. (This Latin version of "one out of many" already had been used on the coinage of New Jersey, New York, and Kentucky.) With a good magnifying glass this legend may be deciphered on the scroll held by the eagle on some (though not all) of the nation's first gold coins: the $5 pieces known as half eagles. The motto was not included that year on the eagle ($10 gold piece), but by 1797 it had found its way onto this and by 1798 onto the silver dollar, as well. The $2.50 gold piece (quarter eagle), first coined in '96, bore it from the beginning.

Although "one out of many" refers, of course, to the uniting of many colonies into one nation, it might have applied equally well

32. 1796 quarter eagle

to the long struggle to substitute one uniform national coinage for the many which were still circulating freely throughout the land. Not only were there all the private, colonial, state, and foreign coins that had been used for years, but there were also some new ones produced since the mint's opening. Among these were the Talbot, Allum, and Lee token cents issued in New York in 1794 and '95 and the Myddelton token cents struck for Kentucky in 1796. And Spanish dollars seemed to be more popular than ever.

Why were so many unofficial coins still being used? Simply because there were not enough government-minted pieces to go around; many people in country districts never even saw any of the new U.S. coinage. Also, since our coins had a little more gold and silver in them than Spanish pieces of the same face value, speculators found that they could make money by exporting American money to various foreign lands to be melted down for its metal, taking their payment in Spanish coins. Not until many years later did the coins struck by the U.S. Mint have the field to themselves.

Because of these complications some coin denominations were not struck for many years on end. Among these were silver dollars, of which there were none between 1805 and 1840. The tallest mysteries in all American numismatics have grown up around the dollars minted just before that long suspension. Mint records for 1804 show that over 19,500 silver dollars were struck that year, yet today not more than fifteen out of all those thousands are known to be in existence. Chances are that most of the rest of them may have been sent to the West Indies or elsewhere to be melted down for their silver; or perhaps they were sunk in a shipwreck which divers of the future will yet discover. No one knows. The handful that remain are either treasured in museums or else are traded between private collectors at fantastic prices.

Almost as mysterious are the silver dollars of 1805. The mint's official records state that only 321 dollars were made in that year, and none of these were placed in circulation. Yet every now and then one is discovered. Usually, however, it turns out to be a dollar of some other year on which the date has been skillfully changed.

Money may have been both scarce and sadly mixed up during the twenty years between the mint's founding and the War of 1812, but that did not keep Americans from spending such coins as they could spare on occasional luxuries. Their first President set them a lively example in this field. In 1793, according to his household account book, he gave $1 for a subscription to the Ladies' Magazine for Mrs. Washington, fifty cents for fishing tackle for Master Custis, eighty cents for two copies of "divine music" for Miss Custis, and $3 for "six tickets to admit the family to see Mr. Blanchard's parachute."

33. *A page from George Washington's household account book*

"Mr. Blanchard's parachute" probably meant "Mr. Blanchard's balloon," which was the famous space capsule of its day. Jean Pierre Blanchard was a daring Frenchman who in 1793 had astounded Philadelphia, then the national capital, by ascending in a balloon from the center of the city to a height of more than a mile and staying aloft for twenty-three days before landing across the Delaware River in New Jersey. He also made some daring parachute jumps. No wonder Mr. Washington was willing to pay $3.00 to see him perform!

In 1794 the President's accounts show a $4.33 item for hair powder and perfume, but when he bought three yards of hair ribbons in 1795 he paid 2/9, which means that every now and then, like many others, he was still using British money. Not all of his expenditures went for luxuries, of course; in '94 and '95 his records show 42 cents spent for "castor oil for sick servants" and 67 cents "for keeping Wilhelmina in jail 5 or 6 days."

Washington did enjoy entertainment, however; his accounts during his second presidential term reveal that he spent $21 for concert tickets, $10 for a box at the New Theatre, $1.75 "to see the elephant," $8 for eight tickets to Ricketts' Circus (the first circus performance in America), and $3 which he "gave a man who had a very sagacious dog for the family to see his performance."

In 1794–95 lesser folk than the President were spending such spare coins as they had on copies of Shakespeare's plays, just published in America for the first time, going to the theater to see Joseph Jefferson act, and traveling between the nation's capital and Lancaster on the wonderful new toll road, the Lancaster Turnpike, which for sixty-two miles had a hard surface of crushed stone, instead of the usual jolting ruts and mud. Over that road many of them fled from the capital in 1797, when a fearsome epidemic of yellow fever caused everything in Philadelphia, including the mint, to close down for a while.

Three years later it was not to Philadelphia that men went when they held office in the Federal Government, but to the brand-new capital city built on the Potomac River marshes and named in honor of the first president, who had died the year before. Soon the book for which all who could afford it were spending their coins was Parson Weems' *Life of Washington*, with its appealing if perhaps unfounded "cannot-tell-a-lie" story about the cherry tree. And spare pennies were given to comically dressed little monkeys on chains, who toured the streets collecting coins in tin cups while their masters, by turning cranks, ground out tunes from their barrel organs on wheels, called hurdy-gurdies.

On a larger scale, the new nation was spending its money on ventures which some people at the time thought were extravagant but which later turned out to be good investments. In 1803 President Jefferson spent $15,000,000 to buy from France the 800,000 square miles of land known as Louisiana Territory, and the next year he arranged for the Federal Government to pay for Lewis and Clark's explorations through part of this newly acquired territory and then on to the Pacific Ocean. A hundred years later both of these achievements were recalled by commemorative gold dollars. The Louisiana

34. *1903 Louisiana Purchase commemorative gold dollar*

35. *1905 Lewis and Clark commemorative gold dollar*

Purchase piece, issued a century after the purchase was made, is available in two types, one picturing Thomas Jefferson on its face and the other portraying President William McKinley, who had been killed by an assassin two years before the centennial coin appeared. The Lewis and Clark gold dollar, showing Lewis's head on one side and Clark's on the other, came out in 1904 and 1905.

Yet not all the important things that were happening in the United States in those early years of the nineteenth century involved the spending of money. One of the most important, in fact, actually prohibited the use of money for a certain purpose: importing slaves from Africa. Another, coming in 1809, the year after the slave trade from overseas was ended, occurred in a backwoods Kentucky family where there was very little money of any kind. It was the birth to Thomas and Nancy Lincoln of a baby boy whose likeness, after he grew to manhood, now appears on our pennies. And a third, beginning in 1812, was the soldiers' joking habit of referring to meat packed for their use as "Uncle Sam's" because the packer's name was Sam and the boxes carrying his product bore the letters "U.S."

But if soldiers joked about Uncle Sam they did not find much else to joke about that year. For they were fighting now in another war with England, and there was nothing funny about that.

Chapter Six

FROM PAPER MONEY TO THE GOLD RUSH

1812–1848

"Mr. Madison's War," men then called what today's history books call the "War of 1812," and most of them did not like it at all. Their leaders said they were fighting because the British had been kidnapping American seamen and blockading American ports, but what the public noticed most was that suddenly everything cost more and that money vanished almost overnight.

To help pay for the war the United States had to charge twice as much duty as before on everything imported from abroad. Of course this raised prices. Meanwhile, the mint was making fewer coins and Congress was issuing millions of dollars' worth of paper money. This worried the citizens, for they remembered what their fathers had told them about the worthless paper "Continentals" of Revolutionary times.

Fearful that they would be left without any money at all, people took to hoarding coins: burying them in the ground, hiding them in a teakettle or an old shoe. Soon there was practically no "hard money" in sight, and any storekeeper who wanted to sell Sir Walter Scott's popular novels or the recently invented lead pencils or iron plows had to take paper money for his wares. One of the troubles with paper money was that you never could tell whether or not it had anything of value to back it up, for it was put in circulation almost as fast as the printing presses would run, not only by the government, but also by banks. Often the banks issuing such currency ran out of funds and closed their doors, causing real hardship for anyone holding their notes.

This is how things were in 1814, when Francis Scott Key, imprisoned on a British warship near Baltimore, wrote his famous song about "The Star-Spangled Banner," and when the British, capturing Washington, burned the unfinished Capitol and set afire the President's gray stone mansion, damaging it so badly that when it was later repaired it had to be painted white to hide the smoke-blackened walls. The next year, even though the fighting was over, the country's currency was still in a bad way. Because of the war's heavy demands, copper was so scarce that 1815 was the only year in our history when the mint did not coin any cents.

A serious fire in 1816 damaged much of the mint's machinery and completely stopped production for a while. From that misfortune, however, some good resulted, for the ruined machines were replaced with new ones much better than the old.

Included in this new machinery was special equipment for producing the sparkling, mirrorlike coins known as proofs. Today, proofs are one of the collector's chief delights, but in those first years of their manufacture they were not sold to private citizens; they were used almost entirely as gifts to visiting governors, congressmen, foreign rulers, and other celebrities. So popular were they for this purpose that in some years they were made in large quantities even when the striking of ordinary coins for general circulation was omitted. This happened, for instance, in 1821 and

1823, when the only cents produced were proofs—well over a million of them during the two years.

When coins became more plentiful after their wartime scarcity they were put to many new uses. They could be spent to make the dark winter evenings a little brighter, for the whaling industry was now entering on its greatest days, and whale-oil lamps gave better light than candles. Another way to brighten the evenings was to buy one of the jolly Swiss music boxes which were being imported in increasing numbers every year. Foods canned in tin could be bought now, too. And there was even a brand-new method of saving money, for the country's first savings bank had just been opened.

It was in the 1820's that authorities at Yale College began imposing fines of from twenty-five to fifty cents on boys who defied the college's ban on playing football. On the quarters and halves that went to pay these fines Miss Liberty now had donned a cap to cover her formerly bare head, but the long tresses down her back were still as untamed as ever.

This same "Liberty cap" appears on one of the rarest of all American coins: the half eagle ($5 gold piece) struck in 1822. It may seem puzzling that these 1822 gold pieces should be so scarce today, for nearly 18,000 of them were issued. Probably speculators made money by exporting them to be melted down and sold, for they were heavier and purer than European coins of the same face value, so they were worth more as metal than as currency. This happened so regularly that Americans themselves hardly ever saw their own gold coins.

U.S.-minted silver coins were scarce, too, not only because they were exported but also because American mines were producing little silver. This was one reason why Spanish pieces of eight and Mexican silver dollars continued to be so widely used in our country until after the middle of the nineteenth century.

Whatever the cause of their scarcity, only three 1822 gold half eagles are known to be now in existence, and of course each is valued at many thousands of dollars. Perhaps we may get some idea of how much the value of our money has shrunk when we realize that when those $5 pieces were only a few years old one of them would have paid for several days' room and board at the world's largest and most modern hotel, the Tremont in Boston, which caused a great sensation when it opened in 1828, with its eight water closets and its 170 bedrooms.

A few years later, a Georgia gunsmith named Templeton Reid began making his own gold pieces of local metal. Gold had been discovered in Georgia in 1828, and Reid had worked as an assayer in one of the mines before setting up his private mint, where he produced eagles, half eagles, and quarter eagles of fine quality. They were inscribed on one side with his name and the coin's value in dollars, and on the other with the date and the words GEORGIA GOLD.

Nowadays, when we consider no coin valid unless it is struck in one of the Federal Government's official mints, it is hard to imagine how these "private gold" issues got into circulation and how they were used. But apparently they were successful, for the year after Templeton Reid issued his first pieces another private southern mint entered the same business. This one was in North Carolina, which, like Georgia, was having a gold-mining boom. It was operated by Christopher Bechtler of Rutherford, who not only struck $2.50 and $5 gold coins but also offered something new: a tiny gold piece worth only $1. Like Reid, Bechtler put no "art work" on his coins —nothing but his name, the coin's value and weight, and the words CAROLINA GOLD. He must have found a ready market for his output, for he, and his son after him, continued to mint gold coins for over twenty years.

In 1833, soon after Reid and Bechtler struck their first gold pieces, the Philadelphia Mint moved out of its old quarters, where ever since 1792 it had had to pay its annual ground rent in Spanish

36. *Bechtler's Carolina gold dollar*

milled dollars. The mint's impressive new building attracted thousands of tourists, and it became even more of a wonder when in 1836 steam power was installed to speed up coin production. Steam engines had come a long way since 1830, when a locomotive had been beaten by a horse in a nine-mile race near Baltimore, but Americans still found it exciting and flocked to the mint to watch the new presses turning out coins at what seemed an incredible rate of speed. A special bronze medal which was issued to commemorate those new presses is still offered for sale at the mint.

It was also in the 1830's that the mint started to make a big change in its coins' appearance. In 1836 an engraver named Christian Gobrecht designed a silver dollar showing on its obverse not the usual bust of Liberty, but the lady's full figure, seated. On the reverse was a graceful flying eagle. These charming pieces never were circulated. Only about 1400 "patterns" were made altogether in 1836, '38, and '39. They have become favorite collectors' items, at high prices.

Gobrecht's figure of "Liberty seated" (which is what numismatists call the series) was placed on dimes and half dimes in 1837, on quarters in '38, on halves in '39, and on dollars in '40. Those

37. *Gobrecht silver dollar (pattern), 1836*

1840 silver dollars were the first "cartwheels" to go into general circulation since 1803. For many years Liberty's seated figure continued to ornament all these coins. The flying eagle reverse, however, was not included; it did not appear on our coinage until the first small cents carried it in 1856, '57, and '58.

Meanwhile, another important numismatic event was the law passed by Congress in 1834 to reduce gold pieces' weight so that speculators no longer could profit by shipping them abroad. After that, Americans began to see more of their own coinage, but not for long, for in 1837 a serious financial panic struck the country, and money of all kinds became as scarce as it had been during the War of 1812.

Behind the panic was a long-standing squabble between President Andrew Jackson and the country's biggest bankers. In 1836 the powerful Bank of the United States closed its doors, and by 1837 most of the other banks were refusing to make payments in anything but paper bank notes. Terrified for fear all their savings would be lost, people promptly began hoarding again, as they had done in 1812. Coins disappeared from sight.

To carry on trade without money is difficult, so for a while business nearly stopped. To fill the void, merchants began printing paper notes in amounts from 6-1/4 cents up. Such paper substitutes for money were short-lived, however; customers scornfully called them "shinplasters" and refused to accept them.

In place of "shinplasters," merchants now began issuing their own brass or copper coins, commonly known as "hard times tokens." Most of them were of the same size as large U.S. cents (a little over an inch in diameter), and they were stamped with various values. People were cautious about accepting them, but they had to do business with *something*, so gradually tokens came into common use, and for half a dozen years they passed back and forth almost as freely as if they had been real money.

A queer way of trading it was, too, for naturally when business

38. Typical "hard times token," 1835

houses and private individuals issued imitation coins at their own expense they often used them to express grudges or as advertising pieces. Therefore a handful of pocket change was likely to contain some pieces praising different brands of shoes or molasses and others calling President Jackson or Van Buren a thief, or the bankers scoundrels.

Just how many different kinds of tokens there were in the 1830's and 40's it is hard to know—perhaps two hundred. Some hobbyists have specialized in collecting them, and certainly they are less costly than most old coins.

Oddly enough, it was while hard times tokens were still circulating widely that the U.S. Treasury Department chose to establish three new mints: one at New Orleans for gold and silver, but not for copper; and others at Dahlonega, Georgia, and Charlotte, North Carolina, for gold coins only. The mints in Georgia and North Carolina, which were designed to make use of the plentiful southern gold and to discourage Templeton Reid's and Christopher Bechtler's private minting of gold, operated only until the Civil War. The war also closed the New Orleans Mint, but it reopened in 1871 to remain active till 1909. If you ever are lucky enough to get hold of any coins of that 1838–61 period bearing a D, C, or O mint mark, be sure to guard them carefully, for they are becoming scarce and valuable. Most of the D mint marks you commonly see, of course, are not from Dahlonega, but from the Denver Mint, which was not established until 1906.

Whether they were using U.S. coins or hard times tokens, Americans of the 1830's and '40's could spend their money in various new ways. Coffee, for instance, was just beginning to come into general use. And there were Currier and Ives lithographs for fashionable parlor decorations, and *Godey's Lady's Book*, the first really successful woman's magazine. In New York people could get newspapers for only a cent; these were called "penny papers." In the late 1840's they could buy balls and bats for a new sport known as baseball, and beginning in 1847 they could purchase adhesive postage stamps. Or, if they were broadminded enough to think women should be educated, they could even spend their dollars on sending their daughters to Mount Holyoke Female Seminary or the coeducational Oberlin College, both founded in the 1830's.

They also could pay to ride on a canal boat, a railroad train, or a steamboat. In the 20's and 30's canal trips were all the rage, and for ocean journeys people still relied mostly on sailing vessels. By the 1840's, however, railroads had begun to be more popular than canals, and boats with sails were gradually giving way to steamships, which sped across the Atlantic in as little as two weeks' time.

One form of travel which kept increasing was that of wagon trains headed west. A commemorative half-dollar, first issued in 1926, reminds us of one of the most famous routes of these migrants seeking new homes in the west: the Oregon Trail. Pictured on the reverse of this coin there is, of course, a covered wagon. Altogether more than 188,000 of the Oregon commemoratives were made in numerous issues over a thirteen-year period. Another commemora-

39. Oregon Trail
commemorative half-dollar,
1928

tive based in Oregon's history is the half-dollar struck in 1925 in honor of the building a century earlier of Fort Vancouver on the Columbia River.

Many other commemoratives have been struck to recall happenings during this period, for a dozen new states came into the Union then, and a number of important cities were founded. Not all of these events had coins issued later in their honor, however; there are only eight commemoratives for states and four for cities.

The state commemoratives are for Illinois (admitted to the Union in 1818), Alabama (admitted in 1819), Maine ('20), Missouri ('21), Arkansas ('36), Texas ('45), Iowa ('46), and Wisconsin ('48). Those for Illinois, Maine, Missouri, and Oregon were minted exactly a century after the territories achieved statehood, but the other four were not. Alabama's came out in 1821, two years after the actual centennial date, and Arkansas's in 1935, a year ahead of time.

Texas' coin was not designed to commemorate entry into the Union, but the winning of independence from Mexico in 1836. Its special half-dollar was first issued in 1934 and was struck in the four following years also. On its face is the single star which marked the "Lone Star State's" flag as an independent republic in the years from 1836 to '45.

Wisconsin's commemorative, struck in 1936 on the hundredth anniversary of the territory's forming, bears an unusual device: a brawny forearm holding a pickaxe over a heap of ore. On the reverse is one of those burrowing badgers from which the state gets its nickname. Illinois' centennial piece features a profile of Abraham Lincoln, Alabama's bears the heads of the state's 1819 and 1921

40. 1934 Texas commemorative half-dollar

governors, Maine's has the state's coat-of-arms, Missouri's shows the bust of a pioneer, and Iowa's displays an eagle on a scroll.

Arkansas's commemorative is curious in that it was issued with two different faces in a single year. From 1935 until 1939 it bore the conjoined heads of Liberty and an Indian. But in 1936, the actual centennial date, there was also another Arkansas half-dollar featuring the state's long-time United States Senator, Joseph T. Robinson.

The four city commemoratives for this period are for Elgin, Illinois; San Diego, California; Cleveland, Ohio; and Bridgeport, Connecticut. Elgin was founded in 1835, the year when San Diego, an old settlement, was organized as California's first pueblo. Cleveland and Bridgeport became cities the following year. Elgin's coin, issued in 1936, honors not so much the city itself as the pioneers who are portrayed on both its sides. San Diego's was struck in 1935 and '36 for the California-Pacific International Exposition. Cleveland's, bearing a profile of Moses Cleaveland, who laid out the city's site in 1796, is more commonly referred to as the "Great Lakes half-dollar," having been issued in 1936 for the Great Lakes Exposition. Bridgeport's, also struck in 1936, is the only one of our commemoratives to feature the likeness of a showman and circus proprietor: P. T. Barnum, whose home was in Bridgeport.

Besides these there are five other commemoratives recalling the years from 1812 to 1848. One of them is the gold dollar issued in 1916 and '17 to mark the erection at Niles, Ohio, of a memorial to President William McKinley, who was born at Niles in 1843. Another is the silver half-dollar featuring a profile of "STEPHEN FOSTER—AMERICA'S TROUBADOUR," through which in 1936 another Ohio city, Cincinnati, called the world's attention to its role as a music center. Although this coin bears the dates "1886–1936," it has its real roots in the years from 1846 to '50, when young Stephen Foster was living in Cincinnati and writing the first of his famous songs. A third piece is a silver half-dollar struck in 1923 on the hundredth anniversary of President Monroe's "Doctrine," which told the world that the United States would object to European interference in North or South American politics. The head of John Quincy Adams, Secretary of State when the Monroe Doctrine was pronounced, appears with Monroe's on this piece.

The other two commemoratives that remind us of this span of our history both have the same subject: the birth of President Ulysses S. Grant. In 1922, a century after Grant was born, the mint issued not only a special silver half-dollar displaying his head and his log-cabin birthplace, but also a tiny gold dollar bearing the same designs. It is not surprising that the little gold dollars should be costly now, for only 10,000 of them were made, but what may seem puzzling is that about 4000 of the 71,450 Grant half-dollars are nearly as high in price as the gold dollars. And why? Because over the GRANT on their faces is inscribed a small star which does not appear on the more than 67,000 others! Place two Grant fifty-cent pieces side by side, and, except to a coin specialist, they will look exactly alike, but one is worth ten times as much as the other—all because of that little star!

Many years before Grant became a famous general he served as an officer in the Mexican War. The treaty which ended that war in 1848 brought much new territory to the United States. It was in that very year in that new territory that something happened which had a tremendous effect on our country's supply of the precious metals from which coins are made. It began at Sutter's Mill in the Sacramento Valley of California. A man named James Marshall discovered gold, and upon that discovery there followed a gold rush, a new state, a multitude of "private gold" coins, and, in time, a new mint.

41. 1922 Ulysses S. Grant commemorative half-dollar (with star)

Chapter Seven

SO MANY KINDS
OF COINS!

1849=1860

Have you ever seen a gold dollar? A $3 gold piece? A $20 gold piece? A silver three-cent piece? All of these made their first appearances in the dozen years before the Civil War—a dozen years which, from the coin collector's point of view, form one of the liveliest periods in our history.

From the very beginning of the California gold strikes there were new developments in the world of coins. The mint seems to have moved with remarkable speed, for hardly had the new gold fields been discovered before the letters CAL appeared on the reverse of some of 1848's quarter eagles. The next year brought the first gold dollars as further proof of the mint's rejoicing at "CAL's" rich contribution to the nation's gold supply.

For years there had been some talk of making gold dollars, but not till California's gold-rush fever gripped the whole country were they actually produced—miniature golden disks less than half an inch across. On their face was a Liberty head wearing a coronet. At first they were exteremely popular; public demand for them was so great that many millions were minted within the first few years after their 1849 debut. But when the novelty had worn off people began to lose their enthusiasm for these tiny coins, which were so easy to lose. It is safe to guess, however, that within the gold dollars' early years of busy circulation many daguerreotype photographs were paid for with them and many were used to gain admission to hear the golden voice of Jenny Lind, "the Swedish nightingale," whose countrywide tours in 1850, '51, and '52 drew overflowing crowds wherever she appeared under the management of that master show-man, P. T. Barnum.

Only a year after the gold dollar there appeared another new gold coin, twenty times as large but bearing the same Liberty head as the smaller piece. Twenty dollars was then a colossal sum; a single one of those double eagles would have paid the steerage fare of two immigrants from Europe to the United States! Therefore it seems surprising that within their first three years they were minted in nearly as large quantity as the gold dollars. This may have been because, with checks still uncommon and paper money unpopular, coins often were used even in large transactions like the buying of houses.

Although double eagles of the 1850's originally were worth twenty times as much as gold dollars, today they seldom cost collectors more than twice as much. This is due to their higher face value;

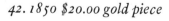
42. 1850 $20.00 gold piece

great quantities of gold dollars probably disappeared from circulation because people treasured them as keepsakes, but few could afford to do this with $20 coins, so they remained in circulation longer.

The years that introduced gold dollars and double eagles also brought the minting of many millions of dollars' worth of other gold coins: eagles, half eagles, quarter eagles, and, beginning in 1854, $3 gold pieces. But these official government issues were only a small fraction of the many gold pieces struck between 1849 and 1855. Gold was so plentiful in California that dozens of different bankers, business firms, and assay offices set up their own small mints and struck golden money marked with values of $5, $10, $20, $50, and various other amounts. There were even miniature bits of gold coinage worth only a quarter or a half-dollar. Some of the private-issue coins were eight-sided or square, but most of them were designed to look as much as possible like regular U.S. coinage, with the familiar insignia of Liberty, eagle, and stars. Oregon made gold pieces of its own, too, and so did Utah and, somewhat later, Colorado.

Today the Federal Government most certainly would object to such private issues as these and would prosecute their makers as counterfeiters, but back around 1850 it actually welcomed them, for there were not nearly enough government-issue coins available in the Far West to meet that growing section's needs. After the government at last established a mint in San Francisco in 1854 the

43. California octagonal gold piece, 1851

striking and use of privately-minted coins was declared illegal, yet private pieces continued to circulate for several years, and they have remained popular with collectors ever since.

By the time the San Francisco Mint was established, California had been a state for four years. Its entry into the Union in 1850 was recalled in 1925 by the striking of a "diamond jubilee" commemorative half-dollar bearing on its face the likeness of a "forty-niner" panning gold.

One thing that many newcomers to California missed badly was the inexpensive mail service available in the east. In 1851 the first class mail rate throughout the older part of the country was reduced from five cents to three cents for half an ounce, and to match the changed price of stamps the Philadelphia and New Orleans Mints began in that same year to make a new coin sometimes called the "trime"—a silver piece worth three cents. Its design was extremely simple, with a star on the face and a Roman numeral III on the reverse. In size it was barely larger than the gold dollar, and it had much the same kind of history. At first it was wildly popular—so popular that in 1852 nearly nineteen million had to be minted. Then gradually the demand fell off, probably for the same reason as with the dollar: the coin was too small and too easily lost to be practical.

Still thinking in terms of three, the mint in 1854 introduced a $3 gold piece. On its face was a bust of Liberty wearing a headdress of standing feathers resembling a crown. This feathery circlet was also placed that year on the gold dollar's Liberty. These new coins were not successful, for they were so much like the long-established $2.50 gold pieces in size and weight as to be confusing. Because people stubbornly refused to accept them not many were issued—only a little over half a million in all the thirty-six years they were made. This is fewer than the total of any other regular-issue U.S. coin, so naturally almost all $3 gold pieces in good condition bring large prices from collectors.

When we look at one of those little $3 gold coins it is hard to realize how much it would buy in its day. At the time the first one appeared in 1854 a few department stores in large cities had just taken the daring step of employing women as clerks, and, although masculine clerks sometimes got as much as $3 a week, women usually had to work for less. That $3 would have provided not only a week's room and board but also a 25-cent theater ticket, a 12-1/2-cent haircut, and a copy of the much talked-about book, *Uncle Tom's Cabin*, with enough left over to buy some safety pins—the latest thing in clever inventions.

Fresh from its experiments with three cent pieces and three new gold pieces, the mint now began making changes in the cent. Ever since the country's earliest days our pennies had been so heavy that people disliked them and often would not accept them. Moreover, copper was so expensive that the mint lost money on every cent it coined. It was high time for a change.

Altering the penny was a slow process, however. For several years the mint experimented with different patterns of various sizes and materials; some were even in the shape of a doughnut, with a hole in the center. Out of all these trials and errors there came in 1856 the pattern for the new small cent, bearing on its face something very much like the graceful flying eagle that Christian Gobrecht had designed for the silver dollar's reverse in the 1830's. The model for the bird on this coin was commonly reported to be a tame eagle that for several years was a pet of the Philadelphia Mint's employees.

Only about a thousand of the new small cents were struck in 1856, along with almost three million of the larger pieces. The new

44. 1856 flying eagle cent (pattern)

cents were small only by contrast with the old ones; in diameter they were no bigger than our cents of today, but their thickness was much greater, and they were still expensive to make, for the copper was alloyed with 5 per cent of costly nickel.

Those thousand or so flying-eagle patterns of 1856 were not issued to the general public; they went mainly to congressmen and others in influential positions. Hence their value today is extremely high.

Something else that happened in 1856 was responsible for a great deal of activity at the mint nearly a century later. A slave mother on a Virginia plantation gave birth to a baby boy who in time was to be elected to the Hall of Fame and whose life was honored by the striking of a commemorative half-dollar. The inscription on the reverse of that commemorative is FROM SLAVE CABIN TO HALL OF FAME, and the head on the obverse is, of course, that of Booker T. Washington, the man whose great work as an educator led to this coin, of which more copies were minted than of any other commemorative except the Columbian half-dollar.

Booker Washington's autobiography, *Up from Slavery*, says that money of any kind, even pennies, was painfully scarce in his poverty-stricken childhood, so probably he had few glimpses then of the coin that shared his birth year, the flying eagle cent. That little eagle, having tried his wings in a limited way in 1856, first flew into popular affection in 1857. Over seventeen million of the small cents were issued that year, compared with only a third of a million of

45. Booker T. Washington commemorative half-dollar, 1950

the large ones. The mint sped up the new coin's distribution by displaying in post offices and other public places a circular urging people to turn in their large cents or their fractional Spanish and Mexican silver pieces in exchange for flying eagles. As soon as large cents were turned in they were melted down for their copper, which is why they are not more plentiful today. Those for 1857, being particularly scarce, always bring good prices in the collectors' market.

The large cent was not the only American coin to make its final appearance in 1857. Also minted for the last time in that year was the half cent, which, like the large cent, never had been popular. For many years before its end it had appeared only in small quantities. To have made it any longer would have brought real confusion, for it was considerably larger than the new small cent, worth twice as much!

In some circles, however, both the half cent and the large cent became more sought-after at this time than they ever had been before, for it was around 1857 that the modern hobby of coin-collecting had its real beginning in the United States. Some Americans were suddenly beginning to realize that if they wanted to preserve specimens of various vanishing species of coinage they had better act fast.

Feeding on this new group of hobbyists was a skillful counterfeiter in New York, who around this time began making and selling remarkably good imitations of the early New England willow-tree, oak-tree, pine-tree, and "N E" shillings and other early coins. Some of these fake coins of old New England are still around to fool unwary buyers, but the 1850's were the time when they were most widely sold, for many collectors then were too new at the game to have learned to be cautious.

Coin enthusiasts in 1857 had a far wider variety of pieces to work with than has today's collector. There were not only the last half cents and the two sizes of cents, but also silver pieces worth 3, 5, 10,

46. 1853 quarter with arrows

25, 50, and 100 cents and gold pieces worth $1, $2.50, $3, $5, $10, and $20—fifteen different kinds of coins in all, compared with only five kinds today!

To add to the variety, there had been two types of half dimes, dimes, quarters, and half-dollars struck in 1853. Some of them looked just like '52 coins, except for their date, but the majority had two arrowheads to the left and right of the date. The mint said the arrows indicated a change in the coins' alloy. Whatever the reason, the two different designs gave collectors some new complications to worry about. There were arrows on 1854 and '55 coins, too, but they disappeared in '56.

Nor was that all, for there were still in common use large numbers of foreign coins, especially Spanish, Mexican, and English, as there had been ever since the days before the United States was born. It was in that same numismatically busy year of 1856 that Congress at last passed some long-overdue legislation: it ruled that within the next two years all foreign coins must be exchanged for American ones; after that deadline they no longer would be legal tender in this country. A man who formerly could pay his barber for a haircut with a Spanish reale worth 12-1/2 cents would now have to pay with an American dime plus two American cents and one of the vanishing half cents.

Not long after this law passed there was a serious business panic. Banks closed down for a couple of months, making it difficult to exchange foreign coins for American ones. As a result the deadline was postponed for two more years. Before that deadline arrived, however, there came several events to cause excitement among the growing army of coin collectors.

The first was the mint's decision (inspired by collectors' requests) to make proofs for sale. Sets of these beautiful coins, which for forty-one years had been available only to celebrities, were now to be sold, in a handsome casket, to anyone who was willing to pay $3.08 more than their face value—$3 for the casket and eight cents for the proofing. Orders for caskets filled with proofs promptly poured in upon the Philadelphia Mint. (No proofs were made in the branch mints.) A few collectors considered it extravagant to have to pay the $3.08 premium, but most buyers of the newly offered sets looked upon their purchases as a bargain and displayed them as proudly as if they had been precious gems—as, indeed, they turned out to be; anyone lucky enough to possess an 1858 proof set today could sell it for a gem-sized price.

The next event in the coinage world was a puzzling one. For some unexplained reason the mint abandoned the cent's flying eagle design after only a little over two years, replacing it in 1859 with the so-called "Indian head" which continued to adorn our one cent piece for half a century. Those Indian-head pennies are among the most familiar of our coins; nearly two billion of them were issued before they were replaced in 1909 by the Lincoln penny.

Late in 1859 and early in '60 the mint made a slight change in the little silver half dime's design, moving the inscription UNITED STATES OF AMERICA from the reverse to the obverse. Such a trifling alteration as this would not be worth mentioning here if

47. 1859 Indian-head cent

48. 1860 transitional half dime

there had not happened in the process a very odd thing: a hundred or so of the 1859–60 half dimes somehow or other were struck with the 1859 face and the 1860 reverse! What this meant was that the words UNITED STATES OF AMERICA did not appear on *either* side; the coins might just as well have been issued by some other country for all you could tell by looking at them. Naturally these "transitional half dimes"—as numismatists call them—are an expensive treasure for collectors. Even when they were brand new they were recognized as something rare and precious, so they were not spent, as were some of the ordinary half dimes, to tip porters on the railroads' new Pullman sleeping cars or to pay for rides on the horsecars which now ran on metal tracks to carry passengers along city streets.

Another exciting development in the field of transportation was the new mail service between the East and California via Pony Express—daring riders who carried letters from St. Joseph, Missouri (the end of the telegraph line) to Sacramento, taking ten days for the trip. Sending mail by this route was expensive: $5 a half ounce when the service started in April of 1860. (Five dollars was a lot of money in a year when skilled shoemakers in Massachusetts were striking over reduction of their wages to $3 a week.)

Later the fee for mail from St. Joseph to Sacramento went down to a dollar, but soon afterward something happened that not only hastened the end of the Pony Express but also closed the southern mints and almost shattered the United States. It was, of course, the Civil War.

Chapter Eight

"IN GOD WE TRUST"

1861-1866

From the numismatic viewpoint the Civil War period was a crowded time. Again coins disappeared from circulation, as they had in earlier wars, and again people used tokens, paper currency, and other money substitutes. New coins were born then, too, and so was the motto that now appears on all our coinage. And the southern mints' closing sowed the seed for future collectors' treasures.

When the Confederate States seceded from the Union they took over the mints at Dahlonega, New Orleans, and Charlotte. These mints made a few coins for the Confederacy, but their usefulness was short-lived, for they had too little metal to keep going.

Rarest and most expensive of the coins they struck, all on United States dies, are Dahlonega's 1861 gold dollars and New Orleans' double eagles of that same date. Dahlonega's and Charlotte's 1861 $5 gold pieces bring high prices, too, but the 1861 half-dollars struck in New Orleans are no more costly than Philadelphia halves of the same date, for over two million of them were minted.

The Confederacy had ambitious plans for producing coins of its own design, and dies were prepared for a half-dollar and a cent, but the mints' closing came before any of these could be issued. However, about ten years later a number of restrikes were made from those unused 1861 dies. These were produced privately, and merely for collectors, not for circulating coinage, but they were eagerly snapped up and have continued to be in great demand ever since.

During those years of conflict it was a rare Southerner who ever saw coins of any sort except a few hoarded pre-war pieces, which were spent grudgingly and only when absolutely necessary. What people *did* spend were postage stamps for small change and, for larger amounts, "bluebacks"—paper treasury notes issued by the Confederacy in amounts ranging from fifty cents to a thousand dollars. There were also paper notes printed by various states and cities, plus thousands of kinds of privately issued tokens—so many varieties that nobody could possibly keep track of them or know whether they were worth anything. In New Orleans, according to the jokers, you could pass the label off an olive oil bottle as money because it was greasy, smelled bad, and bore an autograph!

As coins disappeared the value of the newborn paper currency notes went constantly down. As more were printed, their buying power shrunk. In Richmond, late in the war, a chicken cost (in

49. *Confederate half-dollar, 1861*

50. *Typical privately issued Civil War token (Confederate)*

Confederate money) $50, a pound of beef $15, a bushel of potatoes $80. A gold dollar would bring $100 in paper money.

Meanwhile the North, though not quite so short of cash as the South, was not having an easy time, either. The Philadelphia and San Francisco Mints kept on making coins, but the government and private business switched to paper currency, and many of the newly-struck coins were shipped out of the country, just as they had been in the mint's earlier days. Canada and Latin America had plenty of U.S. half-dollars and quarters, while U.S. citizens had hardly any!

When copper and silver coins vanished, postage stamps found a new use, just as they did in the South. Soldiers leaving for active service carried envelopes full of stamps to spend for small change, and after these stamps had passed from hand to hand for a while and had been jammed in pockets and exposed to rain and perspiration they became so gummy and dog-eared that it was almost impossible to separate and use them. Civilians, too, were finding stamps unsatisfactory as a substitute for coins.

To solve this problem a number of merchants had the bright idea of encasing stamps in transparent-faced holders of cheap metal, with the merchants' ads on the back. Unlike loose stamps, these could be spent and respent any number of times without wearing out.

After the war had been on for a year or so the use of stamps in place of coins became less common, for by that time Congress had authorized large-scale printing of paper money. This new government-issue paper included not only "greenbacks" valued from $1 to $1000, but also "fractional currency" worth 5¢, 10¢, 25¢, and 50¢.

51. Encased postage-stamp currency

(From '64 to '69 there was also a 3¢ note, and from '69 to '75 a 15¢ one.)

So well had postage stamps caught on as money that at first fractional currency was printed to look exactly like stamps. Taking the place of silver quarters, for instance, was a paper note showing pictures of five 5-cent stamps. From 1863 on, however, the Treasury got away from the postage-stamp idea and made its fractional currency look more like other paper money, featuring heads of Washington and of various generals and cabinet officers.

Occasionally nowadays someone comes across some of this fractional currency of the 60's and 70's and throws it away, thinking it as worthless as Confederate paper money and the Revolution's "Continentals." Nothing could be further from the truth, for the Treasury Department will still redeem its old fractional notes at their full face value. To redeem them in this way would be foolish, however, for most coin dealers will pay more for them than the government will.

Also carried and spent by many civilians and soldiers on the Northern side of the lines were privately issued tokens, popularly called "copperheads." Thousands of different kinds of these appeared. They were made of various metal alloys and were about the same in size as genuine cents, most of which were now being either hoarded or exported. To make the likeness to real cents even more striking, the tokens' faces usually bore Indian heads, but on the reverse were business firms' advertisements. Sometimes the issuing firms used the tokens' reverse for such patriotic slogans as "Our Country—United Forever!" or "Death to Traitors!"

Most of this strange assortment of Civil War currency was spent on nothing but absolute necessities; there was little to spare for luxuries while the war was on. Some of the larger greenbacks were used in a way that would be considered shocking today: they bought exemption from military service. If a conscripted man did not want to serve, he paid the government $300, and someone who had less money had to serve in his place.

52. Civil War token (North) with slogan, 1863

Smaller sums were spent in ways that would have been impossible a few years before. For example, there was the thrill of sending telegrams all the way to California by way of the transcontinental telegraph line (completed in the fall of 1861) which had helped to kill the Pony Express. And there were new paperbound books known as "dime novels," dealing with blood-tingling adventures. These were particularly popular with soldiers, who carried the little books in their knapsacks and swapped them with each other.

Some Union Army men managed to send home a good part of their $13 a month pay (this went up to $16 in 1864), but others regularly spent most of it on food, clothing, and luxuries bought from sutlers, the merchants who traveled to army encampments with all kinds of things for sale. One of the items soldiers bought from them in great quantities was that convenient new invention, condensed milk, for which they paid 75 cents a can. Butter (usually rancid) was $1 a pound, molasses cookies were six for a quarter, and indigestible hunks of something which sutlers called pie went also for a quarter. All these luxuries tasted wonderful to men who had tired of their dull army rations. In Confederate camps, however, sutlers' wagons seldom were seen, for the men had almost no money to spend.

As soon as they were mustered out of the army, many soldiers who had saved their pay made good use of it by taking advantage of the new Homestead Act. This provided that a quarter section (160 acres) of public land could become the property of anyone who would stake a claim, live on the land for five years, and pay $1.25 an acre. Thus for $200 a man who was willing to do a lot of hard work could acquire a large farm or ranch. Naturally many greenbacks of the 60's went for this purpose.

In the West, where most of the public land was located, paper money never supplanted coins as completely as in the East. West of the Mississippi people still looked with suspicion on any currency except that made of metal, and even in the war's darkest days they refused to accept greenbacks, fractional notes, and postage-stamp currency. As a result of this stubborn demand for specie the San Francisco Mint actually surpassed its Philadelphia parent in the production of half dimes, dimes, half-dollars, and gold coins in most years from 1862 on into the 70's.

This does not mean that the Philadelphia Mint was idle, however. One task on which it was working was designing and launching three brand-new coins; another was changing the makeup of the cent.

Changing the cent was necessary because of the wartime scarcity and cost of nickel, which formed 12 per cent of every penny. Its price had soared so high that the mint would soon have been losing money on each piece (as it had done on the old large cents) if it had not shifted from copper-nickel to bronze—an alloy composed chiefly of copper, with a little tin and zinc. In 1864, when this change was made, the Philadelphia Mint struck over 39 million of the new bronze cents. They are not all of equal value to collectors, however. The ones most sought after are those that have a tiny "L" under the bottom feather of the Indian bonnet. This "L" (the initial of J. B. Longacre, the mint's designer) continued to be part of the Indian-head cents until they were abandoned forty-five years later, but only a small fraction of the 1864 cents have it.

The three new coins that were introduced around this time were the bronze two-cent piece, first struck in 1864; the nickel three-cent piece, which appeared in 1865; and the five-cent nickel, which followed a year later. Actually the three- and five-cent pieces contained three times as much copper as nickel, but because they had nickel's whitish color instead of copper's brownish tone people spoke of them as nickel, as they do to this day of the five-cent coin.

The two-cent piece, although much sought after at first, later

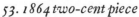

53. 1864 two-cent piece   *54. 1866 five-cent nickel*

came to be so much disliked that it was abandoned after only ten years. But in spite of its short life it has a lasting claim to fame: it was the first coin to bear the words IN GOD WE TRUST, which have since become our national motto. This inscription was the result of many requests to the Secretary of the Treasury from a number of citizens who said that our coinage should carry an expression of religious faith. Two years later the motto was added to seven other coins.

In appearance the two-cent piece was a blending of the quarter's size with the penny's bronze hue, but its design was quite unlike either of them: on its face was a simple shield, with the famous motto above, and on the reverse was the value, 2 CENTS, enclosed in a wreath.

At first glance the three-cent nickel, which first entered circulation in the war's final year, looks rather like our 1916–45 "Mercury head" dime. The size is almost the same, and the cleancut Liberty head resembles the dime's Mercury head. On the reverse, however, the likeness vanishes; the three-cent nickel, like the silver three-cent piece, which still was being made in small quantities in the 60's, features a large Roman numeral III as its chief device.

One reason for issuing this coin was to speed up redemption of the three-cent paper currency notes which had been printed in large quantities. Those little rectangles of paper money were growing sadly worn from use, and the Treasury was anxious to get them out of circulation.

The five-cent nickel had a similar purpose. When it first appeared in 1866 many people resented it, for it was competing with one of the very oldest of our coins, the silver half dime, which the mint had been making ever since 1794. From their very beginning nickels were produced in far greater quantity than the tiny silver pieces; we can only guess that mint officials were already hoping that before long they could abandon the half dimes, as they eventually did eight years later. In appearance those first nickels had little in common with the five-cent pieces we know so well today. They were much like the new two-cent pieces, with a shield on the face and a large 5 in a circlet of stars on the reverse. Like the two-centers, they proclaimed IN GOD WE TRUST.

In that same year of 1866 this motto also made its first appearance on half a dozen other coins: the quarter, half-dollar, silver dollar, half eagle, eagle, and double eagle. Not till forty or fifty years later, however, did it find its way onto the cent, the dime, and the quarter eagle.

Reminders of those Civil War years that brought so many changes in our coinage are three commemorative half-dollars: the Stone Mountain, Antietam, and Gettysburg pieces.

The Stone Mountain commemorative was issued in 1925, when the first section of the Stone Mountain Memorial to the Confederacy and its heroes had just been unveiled in northwestern Georgia, where it is carved from a great granite dome near the mountain's top. The coin's face shows Stonewall Jackson and Robert E. Lee on horseback.

Antietam is the spot in northwestern Maryland where Lee was turned back in 1862 on his first attempt to invade the North. The coin struck in 1937 on the seventy-fifth anniversary of that battle is an excellent example of burying the hatchet, for the busts of the two former enemies—the North's McClellan and the South's Lee— appear together on the obverse, while on the reverse is shown the

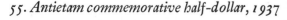

55. Antietam commemorative half-dollar, 1937

bridge on Antietam Creek for which the bloody battle was fought.

Gettysburg's half-dollar, like Antietam's, suggests the healing of old wounds. On its face are the conjoined heads of a Union and a Confederate soldier, and, side by side on the reverse, are the shields of the North and the South. This coin was designed as part of the observance of the seventy-fifth anniversary of the Battle of Gettysburg in 1938, but it first appeared two years before that anniversary.

On hearing of Gettysburg most of us are less likely to think of military leaders than of Abraham Lincoln and his address at that battlefield. When Lincoln delivered his brief Gettysburg speech his heart was heavy because of the strife that darkened his country; seventeen months later, happy that the conflict was over at last, he planned to forget his cares for an evening by attending a comedy performance at Ford's Theater in Washington. During the war most theaters had been closed, but now many a hoarded coin came to light as word of the President's plans got around, and people rushed to buy tickets for *Our American Cousin* at Ford's so that they might catch a glimpse of Mr. Lincoln and help him to rejoice in the ending of the war.

What they saw was a tragic page of history—a page that we can remember when we behold the coins and greenbacks of the 1850's and early 60's, wondering whether some of the very pieces at which we are looking may perhaps have been used to gain admission to Ford's Theater on the night of April 14, 1865—the night when Lincoln was shot.

Chapter Nine

TOO MUCH SILVER

1867=1893

In the plot that killed Lincoln one of those wounded was William H. Seward, the Secretary of State who two years later brought public scorn on himself by paying Russia over $7,000,000 for the vast Territory of Alaska. Most Americans considered Alaska a bad bargain and nicknamed it "Seward's Icebox." Alaska, however, is still with us, which is more than can be said for a number of numismatic arrivals around that same time.

There were, for instance, twenty-cent pieces, trade dollars, Stellas, and the Carson City Mint. All of these had their birth and death during those post-Civil War years which also brought the farewell appearance of six other coins and of paper fractional currency, as well as the striking of the first commemoratives. Altogether it was a very lively numismatic period, and one of the things that made it so lively was the problem of silver.

Silver had been used in our coinage from the earliest days, but our silver supply always had been limited—sometimes too limited for the mint to produce as many coins as were needed. Then just before the Civil War came the discovery of the Comstock Lode in western Nevada, one of the richest silver deposits ever found. After the war's end so many miners and promoters swarmed into the region that soon the United States had more silver than it could use.

One result of this and other "big bonanzas" was the opening in 1870 of a new mint in Nevada's capital, Carson City, close to the silver mines. The Carson City Mint ran for only twenty-four years, producing in that time over 56,000,000 "CC" mint-marked coins for a total value of nearly $50,000,000. It made nine kinds of gold and silver pieces—some of them for only a few years in the 70's. A number of these, such as the '71 and '78 dimes, the '73 quarter, several halves and dollars from the 70's, and the '70 and '71 $20 gold pieces, are rare and expensive. Probably the rarest of all is the 1876-CC twenty-cent piece, of which only a handful are now known to exist, although ten thousand are supposed to have been made. What happened to the thousands of others? Well, that is one of numismatics' many mysteries!

Over four million of the pieces struck at Carson City were "trade dollars," in some ways the most unusual of all our coins. Of all the many kinds of currency that have been circulated by the United States, they alone cannot be redeemed at their face value. Even the Civil War period's fractional paper currency will bring from the Treasury every penny of its original worth, but trade dollars are refused. To know why, we have to know their history, and even then their rejection is puzzling.

Their story starts in the early 1870's, when two groups of American businessmen persuaded Congress that we needed a new coin different from any we had had before. One group, the traders who did business in China, had found that Chinese merchants refused to accept American money in payment for silks, tea, and other goods; the only coins the Orientals trusted were Spanish or Mexican silver dollars. These dollars were slightly larger than ours, and to get them our traders had to pay a premium which took a bite out of their profits. Naturally they disliked this. If only U.S. silver dollars could be as large as Spanish and Mexican ones, they said, the Chinese probably would accept them, and trading would be easier.

Their suggestion was supported by a second group of businessmen, the silver producers, who urged putting some of our excess silver to work by making a special silver dollar a little bigger than Mexican and Spanish ones. The Chinese, they said, would be impressed by its size and would accept it so eagerly that American trade with China would increase.

Convinced by these arguments, Congress passed the Coinage Act of 1873, which directed the mint to produce coins heavier and thicker than standard dollars, but no greater in diameter. These "trade dollars" were to be issued, on request only, to people who provided silver bullion to pay for them. Since they were meant strictly for overseas trade, they were not to be legal tender in the United States in amounts of more than $5. In short, if you bought something here that cost $50, you were not allowed to pay for it with fifty trade dollars.

The Act said that no more of the old-fashioned silver dollars were to be made, but somehow or other nearly 300,000 of them *were* made that year in San Francisco and Carson City. Meanwhile, all three mints got to work on producing a million and a quarter trade dollars, too, with the confusing result that in 1873 there were two kinds of U.S. silver dollars of two different weights. That of the old style showed Liberty in the same pose in which she had been sitting since 1836; in the heavier new-style coin she was still seated,

56. 1873 trade dollar

but was turned in the opposite direction and appearing younger and less forbidding. On the reverse of the new dollar, in addition to the familiar eagle, UNITED STATES OF AMERICA, and E PLURI-BUS UNUM, were the words TRADE DOLLAR and 420 GRAINS—900 FINE, meaning that the coin weighed six one-hundredths of a pound (just under an ounce) and that it was nine-tenths pure silver.

The first U. S. trade dollars reached China at a time when there was a shortage of the popular Mexican dollars, so Chinese merchants were willing to accept American coins instead. Many of the treasures that our great-grandparents cherished were bought with those trade dollars: lengths of fine silk, brass dinner gongs and trays, beautiful Chinese embroidery. American traders were delighted, and for the next several years our mints turned out millions of the new coins annually, although most Americans disliked them so much that in 1876 Congress pronounced them no longer legal tender in the United States. The Chinese were still accepting them, however, and some silver men even suggested that we might also make special trade half-dollars and smaller coins for use in China.

But then the tide turned. Mexican mints stepped up their production, and when plenty of Mexican silver was available the Chinese were no longer interested in the U.S. brand. They looked on Mexican dollars as their own coins; anything else aroused their suspicions. In 1877 our mints made thirteen million trade dollars, but they were a drug on the market. Nobody wanted them.

Something had to be done. In 1878 the Secretary of the Treasury ordered the making of trade dollars stopped. Even so, for five more years the mint kept striking large numbers of proofs, although the Treasury had posted notices in banks and post offices declaring trade dollars void, and the mint had announced that it would not redeem them—not even those made from 1873 to '76, when they were still legal tender. Faced with such warnings, many businessmen naturally refused to take them.

This decision made many Americans angry. The United States Government had issued these coins to its citizens, they said, and if it would not redeem them how could they have faith in their government? For nine years the argument dragged on, with people who could get nothing for their trade dollars feeling more abused all the time. Then in 1887 the government finally gave in. Congress ruled that trade dollars which had not been damaged could be redeemed at their full face value if they were turned in within a given time.

So that, at last, was the end of the trade dollar's strange life as a United States coin. From the collector's point of view it was not the end, however. Nearly 36 million of these pieces had been made, but during the period allowed for redemption only about one fifth of them were exchanged for other money. The great majority either remained in Far Eastern countries or else had been melted down there for bullion. Of the trade dollars that were returned from China there were many that the Treasury refused to redeem because it said they were mutilated. This was true; each Chinese merchant had a habit of using a steel die to punch his own private "chop mark" on a coin's surface as his guarantee that it was genuine. By the time a dollar had passed through many hands and choppings it looked woefully chewed up. Today those chopmarked pieces on which the Treasury turned its back are the ones that collectors value most highly!

Chopmarked or not, trade dollars are not a bad investment for a collector, for they still may be bought fairly cheaply, and chances are strong that their market value will increase considerably as the years go by.

While the trade dollar was living its short and unhappy life, the U.S. Mint was having a constant headache caused by a diet of far too much silver. The Comstock Lode had been only the beginning; other rich mines also had been discovered, and more and more silver was being produced. The silver magnates insisted that more specie should be made from their precious metal, and in 1878 they succeeded in getting Congress to do what they wanted. A law known as the Bland-Allison Act was passed; it said that for the next dozen years 31 million dollars worth of silver coins must be struck every year, whether they were needed or not.

It happened that at this time the mint had just finished making the largest quantities of dimes, quarters, and half-dollars in its history. This was partly to make up for the shortage of metal currency that had persisted ever since the Civil War. There was also a tremendous need for pocket change created by all kinds of new things to buy. One place where coins galore were spent was the hugely popular Centennial Exhibition in Philadelphia in 1876, attended by nearly ten million people. So in '78, when the order for increased silver coinage came through from Congress, very few minor coins were needed, and the mint concentrated on making silver dollars, since none had been produced for home use since 1873.

Year after year millions and millions of silver dollars were struck. So many more of them were made than could possibly be used that great quantities of them have been stored away in Treasury vaults ever since. If you come upon a silver dollar some day with a date in the 1880's don't get too excited; millions more like it are still hidden in those vaults, and every now and then a few bagsful are brought out and put into circulation to turn the clock back nearly a century.

These silver dollars that the Bland-Allison Act forced the mint to turn out by the hundreds of millions are completely different in appearance from the "Liberty-seated" type of dollar that had been issued for thirty-odd years before trade dollars came along. The newer ones (beginning in 1879) are called "Morgan dollars" in honor of George T. Morgan, the mint engraver who designed them. They feature a handsome Liberty head whose striking profile and becoming hair-do look so little like the wild-haired Liberty head on our pre-1805 dollars that you never would guess they were meant to be the same lady.

From 1879 on, Morgan dollars were struck not only at Philadelphia, San Francisco, and Carson City, but also at New Orleans, where the mint closed by war now had been reopened. To celebrate this reopening, the New Orleans Mint was allowed in 1879 to strike proofs—a privilege usually reserved for the Philadelphia Mint alone. Those 1879 proofs with an O mint mark are, naturally, a much-sought-after collectors' item.

The same year that brought the beginning of such a flood of silver dollars also brought the end of the shortest-lived of all our coins: the silver twenty-cent piece. Because hardly anyone wanted this coin, it was produced only from 1875 to '78. Why people disliked it is not hard to understand: with its Liberty-seated obverse and its spread-eagle reverse it looked so much like a quarter, both in design and in size, that confusing the two coins was a constant danger.

Like so many of our coins that have ceased to exist, twenty-cent pieces started out promisingly: almost 1,300,000 were struck in 1875, their first year. But so unpopular were they that in the three remaining years of their existence only 26,000 were added to this total. Ten thousand of these were the vanished 1876 Carson City pieces, mentioned earlier. The remaining '76–CC's are, of course, extremely rare and expensive.

Five years before the twenty-cent piece's speedy death three other kinds of coins had also ceased to exist. These were the two-cent piece, which was used for only ten years, and the little silver three-cent and five-cent pieces. All of these were minted for the last time in '73. The public had not been fond of the bulky two-cent piece, and the trime and half dime had been slated for extinction ever since the three-cent and five-cent nickels' launching in 1865 and '66. Even collectors admitted that it was foolish to have two kinds of coins worth the same amount of money. Yet although the five-cent nickel was probably more practical to handle than the little half dime, many people regretted the passing of the small silver piece which dated back to our mint's earliest days.

Another coinage event of 1873 was the striking of a new group of dimes, quarters, and halves with arrows at the date. From 1853 to '55, you will recall, the mint had added arrows to these coins to indicate a change in alloy, but now in '73 (and also '74) the arrows served a different purpose—to indicate a change in weight. Collectors noticed that there were arrows on the later '73 coins, but not on the early ones. They also discovered that quarters and halves *without* arrows were not nearly so plentiful as those *with* arrows. Therefore they started saving the "no arrows" pieces, which lost little time in acquiring a premium value that has been growing ever since. (The '53 "no arrows" coins also bring a premium.)

In the Centennial year of '76 the Treasury rang down the curtain on the last paper fractional currency. Three-cent and five-cent notes had not been issued since 1869, but ten-, twenty-five- and fifty-cent notes were printed until 1876. They continued to be used, of course, for some years after that.

That was a decade filled with many pleasant new ways for spending money. Croquet, tennis, and roller skates had just been introduced, and baseball had added such novel features as gloves, catchers' masks, and teams of professional players who received salaries and charged admission to their games. Women were buying the recently invented paper dress patterns that showed them how to make elaborate clothes for themselves and their children on their newly purchased sewing machines. Fancy "soda water fountains" were springing up everywhere, and many a nickel, half dime, and three-cent piece went to pay for the delicious new beverages they served. Photographers' studios were becoming more and more common, too; exchanging photos became a popular hobby.

If you were in New York your small coins would pay your fare on the novel elevated railroad, powered by steam, that ran so much faster than horse cars. If you had enough money to go from the East to the West Coast you no longer had to take slow overland trails or a lengthy boat trip around Cape Horn; instead you could travel the whole way by railroad. If you wanted to send a brief message by mail you could buy for a cent one of the new "penny postcards" that the post office first issued in 1873. All sorts of useful things could be purchased for a dime or a nickel or less, as a certain Mr. Woolworth proved in 1878 when he opened his first 5-and-10-cent store, where nothing cost more than a dime. For less than a dollar you had your choice of many popular books recently published, such as *Alice's Adventures in Wonderland, Little Women, Twenty Thousand Leagues Under the Sea,* and *Tom Sawyer.*

In those busy 70's the mint made more coins than ever before, and it also made a number of rarities—some of them so rare that even the wealthiest of collectors cannot hope to own them. Most precious of all are the San Francisco Mint's 1870 $3 gold pieces. Only two of these were minted. Then there are 1877 pennies—so scarce today that they usually cost $100 or more, although over 850,000 of them were produced. For those who like oddities there is the "goloid" dollar of silver alloyed with gold and copper. In 1877 it was made in fairly large quantities as a pattern or experiment, but it never was put into circulation.

Much more famous than the goloid dollar is the "Stella," the U.S.A.'s only $4 gold piece. One of the most coveted of all collectors' pieces, it was struck only in proofs, and for only two years. Altogether 450 gold Stellas were issued, but they were not all alike. Of the 425 dated 1879, there were 415 having profiled Liberty heads with gracefully flowing hair; on the other ten, Liberty's tresses were neatly coiled atop her head. In 1880 there were again ten coiled-hair Liberties, but the model with flowing locks was reduced in number to fifteen. And those were the last $4 gold pieces ever made.

57. 1879 Stella four-dollar gold piece

These rare pieces are called Stellas because the main feature of the reverse design is a large, five-pointed star inscribed STELLA, which is, of course, the Latin word for "star." Encircling Liberty's head on both types are thirteen stars, and between the stars are numerals and letters stating the coin's weight and composition.

Stellas were struck not only in gold, but also in copper, in aluminum, and in a white metal alloy. These were merely patterns, of course. All of them, like the Stellas made of gold, are extremely expensive.

As common as Stellas are scarce are specimens of the mint's next new design, the Liberty-head nickel that made its first appearance in 1883. Ever since its beginning in 1866, the five-cent nickel had had a shield on its face and a large 5 in a circle of stars on its reverse. Now, however, it followed the Liberty-head example set by the Morgan dollar, although the five-cent Liberty was rather grim-looking and not nearly so handsome as the dollar design. On the newer nickel's reverse a Roman numeral V within a wreath replaced the star-encircled 5.

Missing from the redesigned five-cent piece is the IN GOD WE TRUST motto; it did not appear again on our nickels until 1938. Its absence caused some grumbling, but what brought even more complaints was the omission of the word CENTS under the big V on the new coin's early runs. Since the Liberty-head nickel was about the same in size as the Liberty-head $5 gold piece, this failure to mention cents led to trouble: crooks dipped "centsless" nickels in a gold-plating wash and passed them off as half eagles. The mint soon put a stop to this by adding the word CENTS, but not until after five and a half million of the faulty specimens had been circu-

58. 1883 Liberty-head nickel without "cents"

lated. Therefore, for 1883 we have two kinds of nickels: one with CENTS and one without.

Scarcest and most expensive of the Liberty-head nickels for this period are those of 1885 and 1886, the years when many thousands of nickels were being contributed by America's school children to help pay for the Statue of Liberty's pedestal. The people of France had given the United States this famous statue in 1884 as a reminder of the two nations' lasting friendship, but Americans were slow about raising the funds needed for a base. Not till someone thought of asking children to help by giving nickels was it possible for Liberty's pedestal in New York's harbor to be completed in 1886.

Three years later the mint took another big step in its program of cutting down on the wide variety of coins. From 1866 to '72 it had produced sixteen different kinds each year; by dropping two-cent bronzes, silver trimes, and half dimes it had lowered this number to thirteen in '73, and now in '89 it reduced the number to only ten by ceasing to make three-cent nickels and the little-used $3 and $1 gold pieces. (In later years five kinds of $1 gold pieces were struck as commemoratives, but these, of course, are not the same as regular-issue coins.)

The passing of three-cent coinage was not surprising. The original reason for creating it had been three-cent postage, and when the postage rate went down to two cents that reason no longer existed.

People were finding it easier to carry fewer kinds of coins, and there were many things a cent could do that a three-cent piece could not. It could be used, for instance, to operate the coin-vending machines that had just been introduced for selling chewing gum and candy. Newspapers, too, could be purchased for a penny, and in 1890 many an Indian-head was spent to find out just how far a newspaper reporter named Nelly Bly had gotten in her daring attempt to travel all the way around the world in only eighty days, like the hero in Jules Verne's novel.

It was also in 1890 that Congress passed a law forbidding the changing of a coin's design oftener than once in twenty-five years. Probably some such ruling as this was needed, for there had been periods when the designs kept being altered every two or three years. From the coin lover's point of view, however, such changeableness was far more interesting than the dull uniformity that now became the rule. After 1892, all ten kinds of coin except the cent carried a Liberty head. To be sure, each Liberty differed slightly from the others, but the differences were almost too tiny to notice, and the general effect was truly monotonous. We may be grateful that in more recent years the mint has gone in for a little more variety.

In the year when the quarter, dime, and half-dollar joined the Liberty-head ranks the Chicago World's Fair (officially the World's Columbian Exposition) brought a little diversity to the numismatic world by introducing the first United States commemorative coin, the Columbian half-dollar, followed in '93 by the Isabella quarter. To Americans whose regular coins' heads and tails had become an almost solid mass of Liberty heads and eagles the novelty of those commemorative pieces was most appealing, and there were few visitors to the Fair who did not come away with at least one Columbian half-dollar.

One of the Columbian Exposition's showpieces was a six-foot-high copy of the Liberty Bell. It was made from bronze obtained by melting down a quarter million pennies given by school children. Also displayed was a wonderful array of new inventions to tempt Fair-visitors and stay-at-homes alike to part with their gold eagles and silver dollars; among them were bicycles, typewriters, fountain pens, cameras, phonographs, and phonograph records. Some progressive householders were even beginning to invest in electric lights and telephones.

But while the Philadelphia, San Francisco, and New Orleans Mints were turning out more coins than ever to meet these growing needs, the striking of coins at Carson City was falling away to nothing. For some years the only pieces made there had been silver dollars and gold eagles, double eagles, and half eagles. Now even those ceased, and the mint was closed. A feature of its final year, 1893, was the striking of some proofs with the CC mint mark. These are rare enough to be something quite special to own.

The great mining boom's center had shifted now from Nevada to Colorado, where another mint was soon to be born.

Chapter Ten

FAREWELL TO LIBERTY HEADS

1894=1929

In the late 90's men grew quite as excited about the Yukon's Klondike gold strike as their grandfathers had been about California's in '49. Not all the restless youths went to the Northwest Territories and Alaska in search of wealth, however; others were heading southeast to fight for Cuban freedom in the short-lived Spanish-American War. And when the Klondike adventurers came home bringing gold dust, their soldier friends brought from Cuba Spanish silver dollars which no longer could be used as money in the U.S.A.; they served now merely as souvenirs.

Soon after the turn of the century the Jefferson, McKinley, and Lewis and Clark gold dollars were the first commemoratives to be struck at the new plant to which the Philadelphia Mint had moved in 1901. Here for the first time electric power replaced the steam-driven coin presses that back in the 1830's had seemed so wonderful.

By now the San Francisco Mint's annual output exceeded in

value the coins made at Philadelphia, for although Philadelphia produced all the pennies and nickels, most of the dimes, and usually the majority of quarters and halves, the Pacific Coast mint, located closer to the mines, was making the lion's share of gold pieces and silver dollars. Even in 1906, when earthquake and fire caused much destruction in San Francisco, that city's mint turned out coins four times as great in total value as Philadelphia's many millions of minor pieces.

In that same year another western branch mint was added. This was at Denver, Colorado, where for years there had been a government assay office for testing ore from the booming nearby mines. Most of Denver's early output, like San Francisco's, was of high-value coins. No pennies or nickels were made there in those days, and only a few dimes and quarters. Therefore the Denver coins of the early 1900's for which today's collectors are willing to pay premium prices are not the plentiful gold pieces, but the scarce quarters and dimes.

San Francisco dimes and quarters of that period (particularly the 1901–S dime) are costly, too, and so are those from New Orleans. The New Orleans Mint was now nearing its end. With the coming of the mint at Denver, so much closer to the mines, it turned out fewer and fewer coins. Finally in 1909 it was closed for the second time—this time permanently. Scarcest and most expensive of the pieces it struck in its last year is the 1909–O gold half eagle.

This half eagle was one of a number of newly-patterned coins that the Treasury was beginning to launch after years of nothing but Liberty heads. First to appear were the $20 and $10 gold pieces of 1907, a year when the country was in the midst of a financial panic. The $20 piece, designed by Augustus St. Gaudens and called

59. 1907 "Liberty standing" twenty-dollar gold piece

by numismatists the "Liberty standing" double eagle, is sometimes described as the most beautiful of all American coins; its flying-eagle reverse is full of grace, life, and motion. On the first year's issue the date is given in Roman numerals, but probably that "MCMVII" puzzled people, for the dates from 1908 on are in ordinary numerals.

On the obverse of the new gold eagle (also issued in 1907) and the half and quarter eagles, which followed in 1908, the old Liberty heads gave way to Indian heads. On the $5 and $2.50 pieces these really *look* like Indians, but on the $10 coin the head is more like the one on the Indian-head penny: the profile of a handsome woman (probably Liberty again) topped with a feathered Indian bonnet.

The $2.50 piece brought some complaints that it could be confused with a bright new penny. The Indians on the two coins looked not at all alike, and the reverse sides were completely different, but the pieces were near enough in size and color to let an unwary holder sometimes part with a quarter eagle as a lowly cent.

That problem did not last long, however, for in 1909 the mint did a revolutionary thing: after fifty years of Indian-head pennies it came out with a cent of entirely new design—a design breaking the U. S. Treasury's old unwritten law against likenesses of actual persons on any coins other than commemoratives. This revolutionary cent was, of course, the Lincoln penny, first minted on the hundredth anniversary of Lincoln's birth.

The preceding year had brought another notable change in Treasury policy: for the first time in our history, pennies had been struck not only in Philadelphia but also at a branch mint. Those first non-Philadelphia pennies, the 1908 Indian heads coined at San Francisco, are among the most popular of collectors' pieces, together

60. 1907 Indian-head ten-dollar gold piece

with both kinds of 1909–S pennies. (Both Indian heads and Lincolns were made that year.)

Scarcest and costliest of all are 1909–S Lincoln cents with the initials VDB at the base of the reverse, between the stems of the two curved spikes of wheat that form a border. These initials, standing for the name of the coin's designer, Victor D. Brenner, were on the penny in its early runs, but later they were removed. Less than half a million 1909–S VDB's were struck, and with the passing of the years this number has shrunk so much that now they are high in price and hard to find.

Not until 1918 did those famous VDB initials again appear on the cent. This time they were on the obverse, and the letters were so small that you hardly can see them except through a magnifying glass. This lack of initials between 1909 and 1918 is worth remembering in case anyone ever offers to sell you another very rare and expensive Lincoln cent, the 1914–D. If you find on examining this that it has VDB on its face you can be sure that it is a fake—probably a 1944 cent on which the first 4 has been altered.

Public demand for the first year's Lincoln pennies was tremendous. Large numbers of them were spent for one-cent stamps to go on the souvenir postcards (also costing a cent) that were the latest fad. Mounting and saving these cards in albums for display was a favorite indoor sport. Millions of cents went also to feed slot machines in "penny arcades," then at the height of their popularity. And certainly a sizable portion of 1909 pennies, both Indian heads and Lincolns, were spent on buying newspapers to learn the latest news on the bitter, long-drawn-out quarrel between Admiral Peary and Dr. Cook as to which had been first to reach the North Pole.

When you compare a Lincoln cent with the Indian-head type you

61. 1909 Lincoln cent, showing "VDB"
on reverse

will notice an interesting change which is also to be found on all the other new coins that appeared within the next few years. Formerly, the word LIBERTY had been an almost unnoticed part of the Indian's headdress, but now the word became much more important, standing boldly in the obverse field.

The 1909 Lincoln penny had another revolutionary feature: it was the first cent to bear the words IN GOD WE TRUST. This motto, which had been added to most of our coins in the 1860's, had disappeared from the mint's entire output in 1907. The reason for its absence was President Theodore Roosevelt's feeling that coinage was not a proper place for those words. A strongly religious man, he was so outraged at the irreverent jokes inspired by this pious phrase on our money that he ordered the motto dropped. Many clergymen disagreed with him, however, and they voiced their dismay in such solemn protests to Congress that in 1908 the motto came back and even found its way onto the penny.

IN GOD WE TRUST did not appear, however, on the newly designed "buffalo nickel" that made its debut in 1913. This is one of our most striking coins, with its huge Indian head on the obverse, and, on the other side, its great humped bison standing on a mound. Later in that same year this mound was reduced in size, which is why coin books always list two types of '13 buffalo nickels. The bison, like the mint's pet eagle pictured on some earlier coins, was well known to thousands of people who had seen him in his home, New York's Bronx Zoo, where he was called Black Diamond.

One serious defect in this nickel is the location of the date. Appearing on the Indian's shoulder, it is raised so high above the coin's

62. 1913 buffalo nickel

general surface that after it has been rubbed and handled in circulation for a while it almost always wears away; on most old buffalo nickels no date can be seen.

In 1913, however, the dates were still sharp and clear on the millions of shiny coins that still were all you needed to pay for many kinds of things and services. For a nickel you could travel on a trolley car or on one of the new subways or gasoline buses; in many towns and cities a nickel would buy a ride in a "jitney"—an ordinary automobile that carried passengers short distances for only five cents. Or, if you belonged to one of the recently formed groups called Boy Scouts, Camp Fire Girls, or Girl Scouts, you could use a nickel to pay your dues.

Yet, for all its popularity, the 1913 buffalo nickel is not nearly so famous among collectors as are the last of the Liberty heads. There are two reasons for this. One is that 1912 Liberty heads were the first nickels to be made not only at Philadelphia, but also at branch mints; those with S and D mint marks (particularly S) are scarce and valuable. The second reason is that only five 1913 Liberty-head nickels were struck.

Since 1907 there had been newly designed $20's, $10's, $5's, $2.50's, cents, and nickels, and in 1916 the mint carried its sweeping program of change even further by presenting new dimes, quarters, and half-dollars as well. After its long monotony of Liberty heads our coinage was taking on a new look in a hurry.

The dime that made its first appearance in 1916 was a truly beautiful coin. Most people call it the "Mercury dime" because the Liberty head on its obverse is wearing a winged helmet like that always shown on portrayals of Mercury, the ancient Roman gods' fleet-footed messenger. Also reminding us of ancient Rome is the reverse side's design: the laurel wreath (worn by victors in battle) and the Roman consul's badge of authority, known as *fasces* (a bundle of rods with an axe). One thing about this piece definitely is *not* Roman, however; that is the IN GOD WE TRUST motto on the face, appearing for the first time on any dime.

There were two types of dimes in '16; almost as many of the old Liberty heads were made as of the new "Mercuries." That was the period when the multimillionaire John D. Rockefeller was celebrated for regularly tipping his golf caddy only a dime. And for a dime plus a nickel, or sometimes even less, you could put a gallon of gasoline into the tank of one of the Model-T Fords. The cost of these continued to drop down until it reached the low price of about $300 in the mid-20's. A dime would take you into most motion picture theaters, too, although a few of the more deluxe movie houses with "live" orchestras were beginning to charge a quarter.

Probably very few of the quarters spent in 1916 for movies or camera films or any other purpose were of the new "Liberty standing" type, for these were not launched until the year was almost over. Only 52,000 were struck with the '16 date, so they are now scarce and costly. Compared with the new dimes, cents, nickels, and gold pieces, the face of this quarter is not too impressive, but the flying eagle on its reverse is quite as handsome as the one on the $20 gold piece.

In that same year the Liberty on the new type of half-dollar went one step farther: she did not merely stand—she walked! Besides putting Liberty into motion, this piece has another distinction: it is the only one of our coins to show the American flag. Unless you know this in advance and search for Old Glory through a magnifying glass, however, you probably never will find it, for it is draped casually over Liberty's robe and is not easy to see.

The "Liberty walking" half-dollar had been in circulation for only a little over a year before it and all our other coins began to be used for a brand new purpose: to make weekly payments on the Liberty Loan bonds which the Federal Government was urging its citizens to buy to help pay for the great World War. Government authorities were also telling civilians that because of shortages of meat, wheat, and sugar it was their patriotic duty to do without these foods on certain days each week, and that Daylight Saving

Time and the closing of theaters were necessary in order to save electricity and fuel. Another shortage indirectly caused by World War I is that of proof coins. Even before we entered the war in the spring of '17, the mint had stopped selling proofs. Except for 1921 silver dollars, no proofs were offered again till 1936.

Those 1921 dollars were tied in with the problem of too much silver that had been so troublesome for almost half a century. The men who produced silver insisted that the government ought to make more silver coins, even when those coins were not needed. Ever since 1878, when the Bland-Allison Act had forced the striking of millions of unneeded silver dollars every year, our country had had such a surplus of these pieces that in 1905 their production had been stopped. Not a silver dollar had been made since then, and yet there still were many millions in vaults waiting to be used.

Then in 1918 the silver interests again had their way with Congress. The result of their pressure was the Pittman Act, which ordered the melting down of vast numbers of unused dollars for export overseas and the purchase of more silver so that new coins might be made in their place. This seems like an upside-down way of doing things, but nevertheless, over 270 million old silver dollars were melted down! Therefore, despite all the earlier surplus of such dollars, those for some years (such as 1903) are now so scarce as to be really expensive.

The deluge of new dollars to replace those destroyed began in 1921. Almost 88 million of them were made in a single year. Nearly 87 million of these were of the Morgan Liberty-head type that had been coined from 1878 to 1904. The remaining million, however, were something new—"Peace dollars."

The Peace dollar was designed to express the nation's gratitude for the end of World War I. In 1920 a committee from the American Numismatic Association had petitioned the government to produce a piece on this theme as a commemorative half-dollar, but when the new coin finally appeared at the very end of '21 it was not a

63. 1922 Peace dollar

half, but a full dollar, and not a commemorative, but a regular-issue piece. The profiled head on its obverse, symbolizing peace, looks rather like the "Mercury head" on the 1916–45 dime and the "Indian head" on the 1907–33 eagle except for its headdress, which is a diadem of rays like the sun's.

The next year, 1922, brought the strangest coinage record in all the mint's history. Produced that year were over 84 million Peace dollars, over 4 million $20 gold pieces, only 7-1/4 million cents (a mere fraction of the usual crop), and nothing else! It seemed as if the mint, faced with the Pittman Act's demand for such huge quantities of silver dollars, was determined to get them out of the way as soon as possible. In 1923 it produced 56-1/2 million, and after that the number steadily declined, which was fortunate, for the big silver pieces were a drug on the market in a country where, except in certain parts of the West, most people preferred to use paper money.

The surprising thing is that today nearly all dates of these Peace dollars bring premium prices. Probably this is because so many of them never have been put into circulation. Typical of this odd situation was a newspaper account in the early 60's of a boy who made a profit of $35 apiece on a number of Peace dollars he got from his bank.

The surplus of silver dollars and the total lack of most other coins were not the only peculiar features of the mint's 1922 record; another oddity has to do with that year's 7-1/4 million cents. All these were struck at Denver; not a single one came from the Philadelphia Mint, which had produced cents in every other year of its history except 1815. Even more unusual is the fact that on some of the

1922 pennies struck at Denver the D mint mark was omitted by mistake, making them look as if they had come from Philadelphia. Those 1922 pennies without mint mark are, of course, the ones that collectors are particularly anxious to find.

Also struck in the period between World War I and 1929 were a host of commemorative pieces that are listed in the Appendix. Most of these have been discussed in earlier pages, but the five that appeared in 1915 have not, for they all were struck in honor of a single event in our history which had occurred not a century or more before, but in that very year. The event was the long-awaited opening of the Panama Canal, an achievement which greatly reduced the time required for passage from the Atlantic Ocean to the Pacific.

San Francisco celebrated the canal's opening by staging that year the Panama-Pacific Exposition, where visitors had their choice of five coins as mementos. There were a silver half-dollar featuring the symbolic figure of Columbia with a child; a $2.50 gold piece, also showing Columbia, but this time mounted on the mythological monster known as the hippocampus—half horse and half fish; a $1 gold piece having as its device a worker's head; and —most impressive of all—two $50 gold pieces, one round and one eight-sided. Both of these display the head of Minerva, Roman goddess of wisdom, while on the reverse is Minerva's traditional owl. The other Panama-Pacific commemoratives have eagles on the reverse, except for the $1 gold piece, which has only a lettered inscription. Since not many people want to spend $50 or more on a souvenir coin, it is hardly surprising that fewer than five-hundred round and seven-hundred octagonal $50 gold pieces were sold—less than of any other commemoratives in our history. These now command fancy prices.

All told there were twenty-seven different types of commemoratives issued between 1900 and 1928, but after the Hawaiian half-dollar of 1928 and the Oregon Trail rerun that same year no more coins appeared in this series until 1933. This was partly because

64. Panama-Pacific octagonal fifty-dollar gold piece

President Herbert Hoover, in vetoing one of the many bills for new commemoratives, expressed strong disapproval of the growing use of our coinage for this purpose, saying that it endangered our whole system of money. Also, after 1929 many Americans were so worried about how to pay for their next meal that it was out of the question to think of buying coins purely as commemorative pieces.

For the past few years people had been spending money freely and often extravagantly—buying the magical new radios, purchasing real estate (sometimes under water) in the Florida land boom, flocking to movie palaces to hear the novel "talkies," crowding ball parks to see if Babe Ruth would hit another home run, and, inspired by Lindbergh's solo flight across the Atlantic, taking ten-minute rides in barnstorming airplanes. Coins had come to be of less importance than in our earlier years. Few people used them in any but their small dealings. They paid for things mainly with paper: paper currency (just reduced in size from the large bills of the past), paper bank checks, and paper credit. Everything was bought on credit—everything, including stocks on the stock market. And that was the beginning of the big crash.

Chapter Eleven

DEPRESSION, GOLD, AND COMMEMORATIVES

1929=1939

After the stock market's collapse in 1929, when millions of Americans saw their savings disappear almost overnight through bank and business failures, there was only one form of money that some people would trust. That was coins. Since the Civil War, paper currency had come to be accepted as a matter of course, but now the old-time fear of it returned, and with that fear came hoarding. What hoarders believed, apparently, was that if they had enough coins hidden away they might somehow manage to survive, even though banks were closing all around them and millions of men were out of jobs.

The coins they chose to hide were not of copper or nickel or even of silver. They wanted gold. For years gold pieces had been little used except as gifts, but now they were suddenly in great demand. Half eagles soon disappeared; the only ones minted since 1916 were the 662,000 that had been struck in 1929, and these vanished so fast that they are now a high-priced collectors' treasure. The $2.50 pieces were not quite so scarce as the fives, but they, too, seldom had been minted in large quantities (less than 2-1/2 million since 1915) and were not easy to find. The gold that hoarders stored away, therefore, was chiefly eagles and double eagles.

Eagles, like the smaller pieces, had been made in only limited numbers in recent years, and the Treasury had few on hand. In 1932, 4-1/2 million were minted—more than in any year since 1901. Hoarders promptly gobbled these up and clamored for more, just as they clamored for double eagles. The $20 coins had been issued by the millions in almost every year since 1922, but still there were not enough of them to meet the frantic demands of panicky Americans. All the multiple millions of double eagles quickly disappeared from circulation.

At that point the government decided that if hoarding ever was to be stopped the thing to do was to cease making gold coins. Gold had been a vital part of our coinage ever since 1795, but now in 1933—the year when Franklin D. Roosevelt became President—its minting came to an end.

The 312,500 eagles coined in '33 were snapped up so quickly that they are now more expensive to purchase than eagles of any date since long-ago 1798. The mint struck almost half a million double eagles in '33, too, but to keep these from being buried in safe deposit boxes and hidden in bureau drawers the authorities decided not to put them into circulation. Therefore you cannot find a $20 gold piece dated later than 1932, just as you cannot find a $5 or $2.50 coin made since 1929. The smaller gold pieces never were issued after that date. What excitement those long-withheld 1933 double eagles would cause if the Treasury should ever decide to release them!

The chances of this happening are slim, however, for gold has played no part in our currency since the government banned gold coins in '33. For a while after that ruling people were deeply alarmed. They had been asked to turn in to the Treasury any gold coins they possessed in exchange for other currency, and they were afraid they might not even be allowed to have gold pieces as keep-sakes or in collections, but soon they found that this fear was un-founded. The United States has no laws preventing anyone from possessing gold coins of numismatic value.

Many American gold pieces, incidentally, are hidden away in socks and cellars in France, Switzerland, Poland, and other European countries, where they are a favorite form of insurance. In that part of the world they are worth far more today than their original face value.

Despite all the stowing away of gold in the early 30's, hoarders were probably only a small fraction of the population. Most Ameri-cans were entirely too hard up to be hiding any money. The most popular song of the period, *Brother, Can You Spare a Dime?*, was no laughing matter to the millions who had lost both their jobs and their savings. Almost the only income for many of them was what they got from selling apples on city street corners at a nickel apiece. When you see a 1930 or '31 nickel you can be fairly sure that soon after it came from the mint it probably passed through the hands of at least one of those hard-pressed apple sellers.

It was during the depression's worst depths in 1932 that the Washington-head quarter was born. Like the Peace dollar, it origi-nally was planned by Congress as a special-issue commemorative piece, but it ended up by being, instead, a regular-issue coin, taking the place of the Liberty-standing quarter. No quarters at all had been minted during the money-scarce year of 1931. For the first time since the Civil War period, the mint's entire output of coins that year was worth less than a million dollars.

65. 1932 Washington quarter

A long delay in choosing the design was responsible for this change in plans for the Washington coin; it was not ready for distribution until six months after George Washington's 200th birthday, when the commemorative had been scheduled to appear. If it had not been for this delay we might never have had what has become one of the most popular of our coins, for a commemorative quarter would have come and gone in a short time, little known by the average citizen. Changing the Washington quarter from a commemorative to a regular-issue piece required a special Act of Congress. Only sixteen years had passed since the Liberty-standing quarter had first appeared, and, according to law (which has not always been observed) no change in design could be made for at least twenty-five years.

Because of the great depression, the Washington quarter was slow in beginning its career; hence most specimens with dates in the 30's now have a modest premium value. After the piece's initial run of 6-1/2 million in 1932 it was not issued again till '34, for in 1933 the mint produced little more than in 1931, making nothing but slightly over a million dollars' worth of half-dollars and cents. With coins so hard to get, Americans devised various substitutes for money, just as they had done during the Civil War and at earlier periods of financial panic. The "wooden nickels" that you sometimes hear mentioned as a joke really were sometimes used in 1933, having been issued by merchants who hoped that such pieces might help to stimulate their depression-hit businesses.

Hoarding and scanty minting were not the only causes for scarcity of money. Another reason was that people who normally would have paid for things by check had to pay in cash because so many banks were closed. Therefore cash ran short—not only coins, but paper money, too. For one dark week in 1933 every bank in the country was shut by Presidential order in the hope that this would stop the panic-stricken runs which were causing so many bank failures.

During that national "bank holiday" wages were paid and groceries were bought in any number of odd ways. Out of hiding came silver dollars and the old-style large-size paper currency that had been replaced by smaller bills in '29. Also appearing suddenly in circulation were numerous coins of old dates, spent sadly by collectors who, after searching through their treasures, had chosen the ones they could best manage to part with. Mixed with these were pieces of "scrip" issued by merchants' associations, city governments, and financial clearinghouses. Printed on the scrip was always a statement that after a stated date it could be redeemed for a certain amount of money. Luckily this substitute money did not have to be used for long, for most banks reopened within a week or so. Like the depression's wooden nickels, specimens of 1933's scrip form an interesting part of many coin and currency collections.

Those silver dollars that came to light during the bank holiday were all old ones, for none had been issued since 1928. Perhaps their temporary reappearance was partly responsible for the mint's decision to produce nearly seven million new "cartwheels" in 1934 and '35, even though many millions of surplus dollars made from 1878 to '91 and from 1921 to '26 were still stored in vaults. Whatever the reason for their coinage, the 1934 silver dollars struck at San Francisco have a high collectors' value today, and chances are that

66. 1933 emergency scrip

in years to come not only the '34–S but also all the other '34 and '35 silver dollars will be increasingly sought after by collectors, for they are the last of a line which started in 1794. (What happened to Congress's plan to mint 45 million new silver dollars in the mid-1960's is told in the following chapter.)

In the East you seldom see silver dollars now, but they are still almost as common as paper money in some parts of the West, where tourists often are surprised to find such dates as 1888 or 1896 on the sparkling, apparently brand-new dollars they receive in change. The mint-fresh appearance of many of them is due, of course, to the fact that they never have been circulated. Since their coining they have been stored in airtight bags in Treasury vaults.

For coin collectors the big excitement of 1936 was that the mint was selling sets of proofs for the first time in twenty years. Because only five different coins were now being made, these sets were smaller than they used to be, but that at least had the advantage of making them less expensive. A person lucky enough to have purchased one of those proof sets for only a couple of dollars in 1936 has a real treasure now, as any dealer's price list will reveal.

In the following year many workers' pay envelopes became heavier. This was not so much because wages had been increased as because most envelopes now contained coins as well as paper money, for the new Social Security plan required employers to deduct a percentage of each employee's pay for his Social Security account. By now the depression's hold was not quite so grim as it had been, so large numbers of those loose coins from pay envelopes poured into lending libraries' tills in exchange for a bulky new novel called *Gone with the Wind*, while others found their way into the juke-boxes that were beginning to blare forth tunes in thousands of lunchrooms and other public places.

That year of '37 was the one when a faulty die made the buffalo on some of the nickels struck at Denver look as if he had only three legs, thereby giving him a premium value. The following year

67. 1938 Jefferson nickel

brought the buffalo nickels' exit. Seven million of them were coined at Denver, but all other five-cent pieces produced by the three mints in 1938 were of the type that is so familiar today: a bust of Thomas Jefferson, with his beloved home, Monticello, on the reverse. The IN GOD WE TRUST on the obverse is worth noticing, for it had been missing from nickels since 1883, but now it became part of all our coinage. Thomas Jefferson would have been startled at one of the common uses to which those first five-cent pieces bearing his image were put: feeding automobile parking meters, which had appeared on the scene only a short time before the new nickels.

By now coin collectors were beginning to feel somewhat dizzy from trying to keep up with the commemorative half-dollars. For several years after 1928 there had been no new pieces of this sort, but in 1933 the procession began again—and what a procession it was! Forty-four types and dates were coined between '33 and '38, and that was only part of the story, for if you wanted to get specimens from all mints, as many collectors did, you had to have not merely 44, but 80! (See list in Appendix for details.) The only one of these that has not been mentioned in earlier chapters is the half-dollar honoring the opening of the San Francisco-Oakland Bay Bridge in 1936.

There were so many commemoratives, in fact, that before the big parade was over many people began to get heartily tired of the whole idea. Originally they had seemed like a wonderful idea, but they had been pushed too far. Ever since 1935, while they had been issuing from the mint every year in such bewildering number and variety, they had been the subject of many worried notes between President Roosevelt, the Treasury Department, and Congress. The President disapproved of them and the Treasury said they interfered with the regular work of the mint and contradicted the real purpose of our coinage, but Congress kept passing bills for more and more new issues. Some of these bills the President refused to approve, and repeatedly he urged the legislators to make laws doing away with commemorative coins and providing for commemorative medals in their place.

Congress did not do exactly this, but in 1939 it did temporarily wipe the slate clean by killing sixty-odd bills proposing new issues. That served to keep commemoratives out of the coinage until 1946.

Even without this action of Congress, however, there probably would not have been any new commemoratives until after 1945, for the war that 1939 brought to Europe was casting its fearsome shadow over the United States. Before that shadow lifted it was to bring changes in every part of American life, including our coinage.

Chapter Twelve

COINS
BY THE BILLIONS
Since 1939

If large-scale coinage means booming business, then the long depression must have been over by 1940, when the mint turned out fifty-four times as much money as in 1931. The next year's output was even higher: 110 times that of 1931. Yet many people were not happy over this seeming prosperity, for they knew it came chiefly from Europe's tremendous orders for war supplies. And they had an uneasy feeling that sooner or later we might be in that war ourselves.

When we did enter the war, Americans soon found that having plenty of money did not always mean having enough of the things that money formerly had bought. Sugar and coffee were scarce; so were gasoline, tires, shoes, meat, and canned goods. To keep hoarders and speculators from grabbing more than their share of these scarce items, the government organized a rationing system. Everybody had to sign up for ration books, and by the early months of 1943 you had to have ration stamps, as well as money, to go marketing; if you used too many meat stamps on Monday you went meatless the rest of the week.

War shortages affected also the metals from which coins were made. Nickel and copper were needed for armaments, so substitute materials had to be found.

First to be changed were nickels. In 1942, after striking almost 64 million standard copper-and-nickel five-cent coins, the mint began producing "nickels" containing copper, silver, and manganese, but no nickel at all. Over 868 million of these part-silver coins were turned out before nickels returned to their normal makeup in 1946.

A remarkable thing about nearly two-thirds of the wartime "non-nickels" is an initial on the reverse side that never had appeared on any of the many billions of other pieces of U.S. coinage. That initial is "P"—the normally invisible Philadelphia mint mark. The 1942–45 five-cent pieces are the only coins on which our principal mint ever has put its own mark. For that reason most collectors like to have a full set of World War II's P coins, which still are commonly found in pocket change.

Some authorities say that the reason for placing a P on Philadelphia's nickelless nickels and for enlarging the mint mark's size on the '42–'45 San Francisco and Denver pieces was to indicate the coins' change in metallic content, just as arrows were run through the dates on certain 1853 and '73 coins to show a change of content or of weight. This explanation is puzzling, however, because the 1943 pennies, which were changed even more than nickels in content, have no arrows and no oversized P's, D's, or S's.

As copper and tin were both scarce, those 1943 cents were made of steel with an extremely thin zinc coating. (Incidentally, the steel they contain make them the only U.S. coins that can be picked up with a magnet.) Though Lincoln's head was unchanged, they did not look like the pennies people were used to, and almost everybody disliked them. One of the commonest complaints was that when they were new and shiny they could be confused with dimes; every so often someone gained or lost nine cents through such mix-ups.

Since Americans found steel pennies so upsetting, it is hard to imagine what they would have done if the government had gone ahead with a plan it seriously considered around this time to introduce a metal-saving three-cent piece made of glass. From the collector's point of view this would have been interesting, but the glass coin never actually appeared.

Through some unexplained error, a few 1943 cents were made of silver or of copper instead of steel. Occasionally one of these extremely rare pieces turns up and is sold at a high price. A few of the costly '43 "copper" cents have turned out to be copper-plated steel frauds, but others are probably the result of a few copper planchets having been left by mistake in the mint's stamping machines and run through unnoticed with the first steel pennies. It is likewise possible that some silver blanks meant for dimes may have been mixed by error with the zinc-coated steel disks which looked so much like them.

Steel cents doubtless would be much sought after by collectors if they had not been produced in such tremendous quantities during their single year of existence. Even so, they are far less plentiful now than they used to be, and at some future time they may have a premium value.

One thing you never will find is a steel cent in proof form, for 1943 was the year when the war forced a new suspension of proof coinage, which had been resumed only seven years before. This time the suspension lasted six years, and not until 1949 were proofs made again to please collectors.

It is hardly surprising that the mint could not bother striking proofs in 1943, for it was especially busy that year, producing a far greater volume of coins than ever before. Swollen wartime incomes and the rapidly growing use of coin-operated machines had something to do with this increase, but another cause was the changed method of collecting the income tax. For years a sizable number of shirkers had been dodging this, so in 1943 the government started a new plan of withholding taxes from workers' pay. Like Social

Security deductions, this withholding tax meant that an assortment of coins almost always had to be mixed with paper currency in pay envelopes.

There was yet another reason why so many more coins were required. Since the war's beginning everthing cost more. When an item's price went up from five cents to six or seven, more coins were needed to buy it. In 1944 the demand for coins became even stronger, for the cost of living increased 30 per cent within twelve months.

Pennies began to look like themselves again that year, for though the war was still going on, the Treasury was able to get from the army enough discarded shell cases to make its 1944 and '45 cents of 70 per cent copper, mixed with 30 per cent zinc.

Some of those ex-shell-case cents were spent in 1945 to buy newspapers telling of the United Nations' founding, President Roosevelt's sudden death, and the war's ending. (In most places newspapers cost two or three cents around that time.) Roosevelt's death led to the striking the next year of over 344 million dimes bearing his profile. This was the first new type of regular-issue coin since the Jefferson nickel's debut in 1934, and it found its way into the pockets of ex-service men attending college under the "G.I. Bill of Rights" and into the handbags of women who would stand in lines at stores in the hope of being able to buy their first nylon stockings since before the war.

Along with Roosevelt dimes the well-furnished change purse now began to get a sprinkling of shiny new 1946 nickels and cents of normal metallic content. Liberty-walking half-dollars, like Washington quarters, had remained unchanged all through the war, but 1947 marked the farewell appearance of Liberty's figure on our coinage, where the half-dollar had been its last stronghold.

68. 1946 Roosevelt dime

69. 1948 Franklin half-dollar

When Liberty made her exit a fifth famous American took his place as a pocket piece, sharing that distinction with Washington, Jefferson, Lincoln, and Franklin Roosevelt. This was Benjamin Franklin, whose familiar profile adorned our fifty-cent piece from 1948 until it was replaced by John F. Kennedy's in 1964. Quite as interesting as the obverse of the Franklin half-dollar is its striking reverse, featuring a mammoth Liberty Bell flanked by a tiny standing eagle.

Those early Franklin halves are an excellent example of the way in coin collecting you never can predict just what is or is not going to be valuable. Nearly twice as many fifty-cent pieces were struck at the Philadelphia Mint in 1949 as in 1948, so you naturally would think that the '48 ones would be more sought after than the '49s. But exactly the reverse is true: if you have a 1949 half-dollar without a mint mark you are the lucky possessor of a piece for which dealers will pay several times as much as for the coin issued the preceding year.

One of the disturbing things about the new half-dollars and all other coins at this period was that they would buy only about half as much as coins of the same face value would buy before the war. Wages had more than doubled since 1939, but meanwhile prices had nearly doubled, too.

Still, people certainly were spending far greater shares of their income on luxuries than they had during the depression. For one thing, they were buying millions and millions of television sets and phonograph records. Also, when they were in a hurry to drive to distant points they began using the newly-built toll roads; toll booths along these turnpikes collected millions of dollars in coins.

The Franklin pieces were not the only half-dollars to enter coinage history in the late '40s and early '50s. Also struck at the mint during those years were three commemoratives, the first to appear since 1939. Two of these made their appearance in 1946, along with the first Roosevelt dimes. They are the Iowa Centennial piece and the coin honoring Booker Washington, both mentioned earlier. The latter of these became a repeater, coming annually from the mints until 1951, when it was succeeded by another repeater, the George Washington Carver-Booker T. Washington commemorative, which had thirteen dates or mint marks, ranging from '51 to '54. The inscription on the reverse of the Carver-Washington coin, AMERICANISM—FREEDOM AND OPPORTUNITY FOR ALL, struck the keynote for the growth of civil rights for Negroes that was to follow within the next few years.

Although the Carver-Washington piece ran up an impressive sale, it had to compete with increasing rumbles of official disapproval, even stronger than those heard in the '30s. In addition to pointing out that commemorative coins were an abuse of our coinage, being designed chiefly for sale at a profit rather than for use as a medium of exchange, the Treasury Department complained that the mint had had to melt down, unsold, nearly half of the over eighteen million commemoratives it had produced. This showed, the Treasury said, that the public was not nearly so much interested in most of these as their sponsors claimed it was.

When President Harry Truman signed the bills providing for the Iowa and Booker Washington coins he stated strongly his hope that these would be the last. Later, when he vetoed several bills authorizing additional commemoratives, he observed that if we were to note with special coins all the distinguished persons and events our nation has had "we would be starting down an endless path."

70. 1954 Carver-Booker Washington commemorative half-dollar

Next of the Presidents to try to stop the flood of commemoratives was Dwight D. Eisenhower, who vetoed three bills for new commemoratives, saying he knew from earlier Presidents' experience that if he approved these he would be expected to approve dozens of others—some of them of only local importance. Like previous Presidents, he urged that Congress commemorate special occasions by having the Treasury issue medals instead of coins. (Medals, of course, are not legal tender.)

That is why, when Alaska and Hawaii were admitted as our 49th and 50th states in 1959 and 1960, "souvenir dollars" were issued in their honor. In some ways these are like commemorative coins, but a very important difference is that they cannot be used as money. They are merely what the Treasury Department calls "private medals," of which nearly two hundred different kinds have been issued in the course of our history. (Included among them are medals featuring each of our Presidents.)

No commemorative coins have appeared since the last run of the Carver-Washington type in 1954. It is too soon, however, to say for sure that these were the last of the series, for there have been several earlier periods when commemoratives have been revived after everyone thought they were dead.

The year following the last Carver-Washington issue brought two important numismatic events. One was the passage of a law requiring inclusion of "In God we trust" on all United States money. This motto was already appearing on all our coins, of course, but now it never can be omitted from new designs unless the law is changed. The other event of that year, and a rather sad one, was the closing of the San Francisco Mint.

For over a century this busy branch mint had played a big part in providing our money supply, turning out more than two and a half billion dollars' worth of coins mint-marked S. Its greatest period had been during the days of gold; it produced more gold coinage than any other mint. But now the methods of striking coins had improved so greatly that only two mints seemed to be needed, and

San Francisco's was the one chosen to go. Dimes and cents were the only 1955 pieces to bear the familiar S; when you see one of these, remember that it was made by men and women who were about to lose their jobs in what had been one of San Francisco's important businesses since the city's earliest days. After the mint's closing, there was a growing demand for coins struck during its later years.

To understand why fewer mints are required today than in the past, all you need to do is compare the output for 1956 with the output for a century earlier. In 1856 there were five mints: Philadelphia, New Orleans, Charlottte, Dahlonega, and San Francisco. All of these together turned out less than 30 million coins during the year. But in 1956 only two mints, Philadelphia and Denver, produced over one billion, 800 million coins. In short, with modern machinery two mints did more than sixty times as much work as five had done a hundred years before! And in the 1964–65 fiscal year they dwarfed the '56 figures by issuing eight billion coins!

Even this huge increase, however, could not keep pace with the ever-mounting demand for more coins, so in 1965 not only was a start made on building a new and bigger mint in Philadelphia but also the Treasury Department put the closed San Francisco Mint back to work on what was called "a temporary emergency basis."

The year 1965 brought to U.S. coinage other sweeping changes that were even more important than the expansion in minting facilities. These were all ordered by a surprising piece of legislation known as the Silver Saving Coinage Act of 1965.

Surprising? Yes, for only a year or so earlier hardly anyone would have dared to predict that Congress would pass and the President would sign legislation ordering the first major alteration in U.S. coinage policy since the opening of the mint in 1792. This all came about because of the alarming scarcity of silver.

Always the coins of the United States had contained metals that were worth just about what their printed legends said, but now the mint was instructed to make them of metals worth only a small fraction of their face value. Quarters and dimes, instead of being 90 per cent silver, were altered to what the newspapers enjoyed calling a "sandwich" of nickel and copper—a sandwich whose telltale copper-toned filling showed around the rim. The nickel-copper combination was decided on, after much experimenting, because coins made of this mixture would function properly—as various other metals or materials would not—in the many millions of vending machines and coin-box telephones that played such an important part in American living.

Half-dollars, meanwhile, suffered a lesser cut in actual value, being reduced from 90 per cent silver to 40 per cent, beginning in 1966. Having no copper core, their appearance was little changed, unlike that of the quarters and dimes.

Cheapening of metallic value was only one of the startling features of that 1965 Coinage Act. Just as important (to coin collectors, at least) were the rulings that for at least five years there were to be no mint marks or proof sets and also that, no matter in what year coins were struck, they all should bear the 1965 date. This last rule seems to prove that history really does repeat itself, if you will remember New England's seventeenth century pine, willow, and oak tree coinage which bore the date of 1652 for thirty-five years!

Why all these tremendous changes? There were two main reasons. First was the serious shortage of silver, due in part to industry's greatly increased demand for this particular metal, which is especially important in photography and electronics. Those who planned the law reasoned that unless silver was removed from coins, or greatly reduced, its price would rise so high that speculators would soon start melting coins to make a profit from their silver content, just as so many speculators had done in the early days of U.S. coinage.

There was another reason, however, for the Treasury's wanting to turn over such an entirely new leaf: that was the desire to discourage collectors from holding onto large numbers of coins and thus keeping them out of circulation. Mint marks, proof sets, and coins dated differently for each new year—all of these are among coin collectors' delights; all are part of the wonderful variety of earmarks that make collecting such a fascinating game. The very fact that the framers of such a major piece of legislation would go out of their way to prevent collectors from pursuing their hobby gives a fair idea of how large and active the army of collectors had grown.

One other thing about the 1965 Act that should be mentioned was its provision that no silver dollars could be produced for at least five years—a prohibition that followed by only a year Congress's vote (approved by the President) to manufacture 45 million new dollars of silver! It was the Congressmen from the silver-mining states of the West, of course, who sponsored the new-dollar plan of 1964, but a year later they had to bow before the arguments of their opponents, who pointed out that hundreds of millions of silver dollars were already in hoarding, and that if forty-five million new ones were to be minted they were almost certain to suffer the same fate—and this at a time when the nation's silver supply was shrinking to a dangerously low point. So the proposed new silver dollars, like 90-per cent silver quarters and dimes, fell victim to the silver shortage and to the constant pressure for more and yet more coins.

Why is it that we need so many more coins today than formerly? Our population is larger, of course, but that is only part of the reason why banks and stores keep running out of change despite all the billions of U.S. coins there are in circulation. Think how many extra coins are required by the hundreds of kinds of vending machines and other coin-operated devices! And by odd-priced transit fares and newspapers that call for a steady stream of pennies as change, as do sales taxes of all kinds and the habit merchants have of pricing things at $2.98 or $1.49 instead of $3.00 or $1.50!

There is no doubt that certain types of collectors are partly to blame for coin shortages. Thousands of rolls of newly minted pieces are kept out of circulation by dealers and hobbyists who hope to sell them later at a profit. There are also the many people whose misguided hoarding made it just about impossible to obtain Kennedy half-dollars for a long time after they first appeared in 1964, just as it has so often made pennies scarce. (The Kennedy halves were issued, by the way, only sixteen years after the Franklin halves first appeared, so there had to be an amendment made in the 1890 law that required a twenty-five-year interval between changes of design.)

Usually hoarding is based on rumors, and often the rumors turn out to be false. For instance, in 1959, when the Lincoln Memorial first took its place on the cent's reverse side, the rumor got around that only a small number of new cents would be made. People promptly pounced upon them and hid them, and not till after the rumor had been proved completely unfounded—almost two billion cents were struck that year—did those hoarded early-'59 pennies begin to filter back into circulation.

There was similar excitement in 1960 about the small "o" in the penny's UNITED STATES oF AMERICA inscription and also about the small "60" in the dates of the first million or so cents struck. The small "o" pieces soon proved to be worth absolutely nothing above face value, and the small "60's" were the subject of dozens of newspaper articles, some stating that they were worth $8 apiece and others saying they were of no special worth. Some collectors who managed to get hold of one or two of these are still holding onto them, convinced that some day they will have substantial premium value.

That is how it always is in coin collecting and probably always will be. You save a piece that may or may not bring you a profit, and, whether it does so or not, you have fun doing it, for financial gain is only one small part of coin collecting's fascination. The thing that matters most is the part coins play in making history come alive.

Spanish pieces of eight, pine tree shillings, Continental dollars, hard times tokens, trade dollars, steel cents, Kennedy half-dollars recalling the tragedy of the young President's assassination—all of these bring to us vivid pictures of the times in which they were coined and the people who used them. How much will people in the centuries to come be able to tell about *our* times from the coins we leave behind us?

APPENDIX

UNITED STATES
COMMEMORATIVE COINS

Name of Coin	Date of Issue	Date Commemorated
Silver Half-Dollars		
Columbian	1892–93	1492
Panama-Pacific Exposition	1915	1904–14
Illinois Centennial	1918	1818
Maine Centennial	1920	1820
Pilgrim Tercentenary	1920–21	1620
Alabama Centennial	1921	1819
Missouri Centennial	1921	1821
Grant Centennial	1922	1822
Monroe Doctrine Centennial	1923	1823
Huguenot-Walloon Tercentenary	1924	1624
California Diamond Jubilee	1925	1850
Fort Vancouver Centennial	1925	1825
Lexington-Concord Sesquicentennial	1925	1775
Stone Mountain Memorial	1925	1861–65
Independence Sesquicentennial	1926	1776
Oregon Trail Memorial	1926, '28, '33, '34, '36–'39	19th century
Vermont— Battle of Bennington	1927	1777
Hawaii—Captain Cook	1928	1778
Daniel Boone Bicentennial	1934–38	1734
Maryland Tercentenary	1934	1634
Texas Centennial	1934–38	1836
Arkansas Centennial	1935–39	1836

Name of Coin	Date of Issue	Date Commemorated
Silver Half-Dollars (Continued)		
Connecticut Tercentenary	1935	1635
Hudson	1935	1609 & 1785
Old Spanish Trail	1935	1528–35
San Diego—California-Pacific Exposition	1935–36	1835
Albany	1936	1614 & 1686
Bridgeport Centennial	1936	1836
Cincinnati Music Center	1936	1848–50 & 1886
Columbia Sesquicentennial	1936	1786
Delaware Tercentenary	1936	1638
Gettysburg 75th Anniversary	1936	1863
Great Lakes Exposition (Cleveland)	1936	1836
Long Island Tercentenary	1936	1636
Lynchburg Sesquicentennial	1936	1786
Norfolk Bicentennial	1936	1636 & 1736
Pioneer (Elgin)	1936	1673 & 1835
Rhode Island	1936	1636
Robinson (Arkansas)	1936	1836
San Francisco—Oakland Bay Bridge	1936	1936
Wisconsin Territorial Centennial	1936	1836
York County	1936	1636
Antietam 75th Anniversary	1937	1862
Roanoke Island Colonization	1937	1587–91
New Rochelle	1938	1688
Iowa Centennial	1946	1846
Booker T. Washington	1946–51	1856–1915
George W. Carver—Booker T. Washington	1951–54	1864–1943 1856–1915

NAME OF COIN	DATE OF ISSUE	DATE COMMEMORATED
Silver Quarter		
Isabella— Columbian Quarter Dollar	1893	1492–93
Silver Dollar		
Lafayette Dollar	1900	1777–81
Gold Dollars		
Louisiana Purchase Exposition (two types)	1903	1803
Lewis and Clark Expedition	1904–05	1803–06
Panama-Pacific Exposition	1915	1904–14
McKinley Memorial	1916–17	1843
Grant Centennial	1922	1822
$2.50 Gold Pieces		
Panama-Pacific Exposition	1915	1904–14
Independence Sesquicentennial	1926	1776
$50 Gold Pieces		
Panama-Pacific Exposition (round)	1915	1904–14
Panama-Pacific Exposition (octagonal)	1915	1904–14

ABBREVIATIONS FOUND IN NUMISMATICS

AE—Copper

AR—Silver

Ars.—Arrows

AU or AV—Gold

B—Brass

Br.—Bronze

Bril.—Brilliant

C—Copper (also sometimes
Common)

CAL—California gold

C-N—Copper-nickel

Diad.—Diademed

Drap.—Drapery

Ed.—Edge

EF—Extra fine

F—Fine

F.D.C.—Fleur-de-coin, or
Uncirculated

Fr.—Fair

G—Good (also Gold)

IH or Ind. HD.—Indian head

l.—Left (as seen by the viewer)

Laur.—Laureated

Let.—Lettered

Lg.—Large

Lib.—Liberty

MM—Mint mark

N—Nickel

NE—New England

Ob. or Obv.—Obverse

Ov.—Over

Perf.—Perfect

Pf.—Proof

Pl.—Plain

Pr.—Proof

r.—Right (as seen by viewer)

R—Rare

Rev.—Reverse

RR—Very rare

RRR—Extremely rare

Rx.—Reverse

S—Silver

Sc.—Scarce

Sm.—Small

T or Ty.—Type

U or Unc.—Uncirculated

Var.—Variety

VF—Very fine

VG—Very good

XF—Extra fine

MINT MARKS

C —Charlotte, N.C. (1838–61)
CC—Carson City, Nev. (1870–93)
D —Dahlonega, Ga. (1838–61)
D —Denver, Colo. (1906———)
O —New Orleans, La. (1838–61, 1871–1909)
P —Philadelphia, Pa. (1792———). *Seldom used.*
S —San Francisco, Calif. (1854–1955)

TERMS USED IN COIN COLLECTING

ALLOY—A mixture of two or more metals.

ALTERED DATE—A coin whose date has been changed to make it appear rarer than it really is.

ARROWS AT DATE—Term used to describe various U.S. silver coins of 1853–55 and 1873–74 with arrowheads on either side of date to indicate changes in composition or weight.

ASSAY—Examination of coins and alloys to check on purity, weight, and consistency.

BANK NOTE—Paper currency, recognized legally as money, but issued by a bank, not by the government.

BARBER TYPE—Half-dollar, quarter, and dime designed by Charles E. Barber, mint engraver; first issued in 1892.

BAR CENT—Undated copper coin with thirteen horizontal bars on reverse, probably struck in England in early 1780's for use in United States.

BILLON—Alloy with more copper, tin, or other base metal than silver.

BIT—The Spanish reale or real, valued at 1/8 peso or Spanish dollar. Also one of eight wedge-shaped pieces cut from the peso and used as money.

BLANK—Piece of metal of coin size, but unstamped. (Same as *flan.*)

BRILLIANT—Term describing coin in uncirculated condition.

BROCKAGE—A misstruck coin, usually having obverse design impressed backward on the reverse.

BROKEN BANK NOTE—Currency which is worthless because bank issuing it is no longer solvent.

BROKEN DIE—Faulty surface on coin, caused by cracked or worn die.

BROKEN DOLLARS—Coins (generally Spanish) of less than a dollar's value, used in trade with Far East.

BRONZE—Alloy of copper with tin and sometimes other elements.

BUFFALO TYPE—Numismatic term for 1913–38 five-cent piece, also known as *Indian-head nickel.*

BULLION—Uncoined metal.

BUST—Head and neck of a figure.

CAROLUS—Spanish dollar with head of King Charles III, widely used in American Colonies.

CARTWHEEL—Slang for silver dollar. Also English 1797 copper two-pence weighing two ounces and bearing head of George III.

CAST—A copy molded in imitation of a genuine coin.

CENT—Small copper coin of many countries, including U.S.; usually 1/100 of the standard monetary unit. (See also *large cent* and *small cent.*)

CHAIN TYPE—Numismatic term for 1793 cent with circle of fifteen joined links on reverse.

CHOP MARKS—Symbols stamped on coins (chiefly in China) to guarantee genuineness.

CIRCA—Latin for "about"; often used in catalog descriptions of coins of uncertain date.

CIVIL WAR TOKEN—Privately issued copper piece used as money during Civil War to make up for lack of mint-struck coins.

CLIPPED—Coin from which metal has been trimmed around edges.

COB MONEY—Crudely made old Spanish coins of irregular shape.

COMMEMORATIVE COIN—A coin issued in limited numbers to mark or honor a certain occasion or person.

CONCAVE—Hollowed or depressed below main surface.

CONJOINED—Two heads overlapping.

CONTINENTAL—Common term for paper currency printed by order of Continental Congress during American Revolution.

CONTINENTAL DOLLAR—Large coin of pewter, brass, or silver struck by order of Continental Congress in 1776.

CONVEX—Raised in relief above main surface.

COPPERHEAD—Same as *Civil War token.*

COUNTERFEIT—Imitation of a coin, made with intention of deceiving.

COUNTERMARK—Stamp or device punched on a coin to change its value or source.

CROWN—Any dollar-sized coin bearing a crown, especially a British silver piece worth five shillings.

CUARTO—Spanish copper one-fourth-reale piece, first issued in late fifteenth century.

CURRENCY—A commonly accepted medium of exchange, including coins, tokens, paper money, and sometimes such other things as wampum, rings, etc.

CUT DOLLAR—Portion of a Spanish piece of eight that has been cut into *bits* or other parts.

d.—Abbreviation for the English penny.

DENARIUS—Roman silver coin, the "penny" of the New Testament; ancestor of U.S. dime.

DENIER—Minor coin used in France's colonies.

DEVICE—Chief design on a coin.

DIADEMED—Numismatic term for a head arrayed with headband, laurel wreath, or emblem of authority.

DIE—Engraved hard-metal impression of a design, used for striking coins.

DIME—U.S. silver or silver-alloy ten-cent piece, issued in all but fifteen years since 1796.

DINGE—A blunt dent in a coin.

DISME—Old form of word *dime*, used at time of U.S. Mint's founding.

DOLLAR—Standard monetary unit of U.S. and various other countries, usually worth one hundred cents. Also (in U.S.) a paper currency note of a dollar's value. See also *gold dollar*, *silver dollar*, and *trade dollar*.

DOUBLE EAGLE—U.S. gold coin of $20 face value, struck in all but three years from 1850 through 1933.

DOUBLE-STRUCK—Old hand-struck coin that has shifted between hammer blows so that markings are duplicated.

DOUBLOON—Large Spanish or Spanish-American gold coin, equal to sixteen silver dollars.

DUCAT—A coin (usually gold, but sometimes silver) of various European countries, commoner in the past than today.

DUCATOON—Dollar-sized Dutch coin of seventeenth and eighteenth centuries.

EAGLE—U.S. $10 gold piece, issued 1795–1804, 1838–1916, and irregularly from 1920 through 1933. Also U.S. national bird, reproduced as reverse device on many coins.

ÉCU—French coin of American colonial period, first of gold, later of silver. Silver écu was about the size of silver dollar.

ELECTROTYPE—Exact copy of a coin, impressed on thin shell of genuine metal weighted with cheap filling.

ELECTRUM—A natural alloy of gold and silver.

ELEPHANT COIN—Coin or token with elephant design, struck in England in 1690's for British colonies.

EMERGENCY SCRIP—Paper medium of exchange issued by local governments or private concerns at times when official money is scarce.

ENCASED POSTAGE STAMPS—Stamps in transparent mica frames, used instead of scarce metal coins during Civil War.

E PLURIBUS UNUM—Legend on U.S. coins, meaning "one out of many."

ESCUDO—Spanish gold coin worth about $2, frequently used in American Colonies.

EXCELENTE—Spanish gold coin of time of Columbus.

EXERGUE—Surface of coin beneath main device, usually inscribed with date.

EXPERIMENTAL PIECES—Patterns or coins which introduce changes (either in design or in metal) from usual coinage.

FACE—Same as *obverse*.

FACE VALUE—Value of a coin specified by the mint.

FAIR—Descriptive term for a well-worn coin on which date and inscription are still visible.

FARTHING—Until recently a copper or bronze coin of Great Britain worth one-fourth penny.

FASCES—Bundle of rods and an axe symbolizing a magistrate's authority in ancient Rome. Reverse device of U.S. "Mercury" dime, 1916–45.

FIELD—Portion of coin's surface having no device or inscription.

FILLET HEAD—Numismatic term for U.S. Liberty-head coin having hair tied with band.

FINE—Excellent condition, very slightly worn, but sharp in details. Also (in describing metal) free from impurity.

FINENESS—Proportion of pure metal in a piece of gold or silver, expressed in thousandths, with 1000 standing for pure metal.

FLAN—Blank disk of metal on which a coin is struck. (Same as *blank* or *planchet*.)

FLEUR-DE-COIN—Same as *uncirculated*.

FLORIN—Coin with a lily device, originated in thirteenth century Florence and widely imitated later by other countries.

FLOWING HAIR—Numismatists' term for U.S. coin bearing Liberty head with free-hanging hair.

FLYING EAGLE—First U.S. small cent, issued 1856-58.

FRACTIONAL MONEY—Coins or paper money of less than a dollar in face value.

FRANC—The monetary unit of France.

FREAK—A misstruck coin, differing in some way from the usual coin of its type. (Same as *mint error*.)

FRANKLIN HALF-DOLLAR—U.S. silver fifty-cent piece with bust of Benjamin Franklin on obverse.

FUGIO CENT—First coin issued by U.S. after Revolution's end. Dated 1787, it has legend "FUGIO" on obverse.

GEM—Dealers' term for a rare coin in perfect condition.

GOBRECHT DOLLAR—Uncirculated silver dollar pattern of 1836 and 1838–39, designed by August Gobrecht.

GOLD DOLLAR—Small U.S. gold coin, issued in regular coinage 1849–89 and in several commemoratives.

GOLD ORDER—Executive order issued March 16, 1933, by President F.D. Roosevelt, stopping coinage of gold and removing gold coins from U.S. circulation.

GOLOID DOLLAR—Pattern dollar of silver, gold, and copper, struck experimentally in 1877, but never circulated.

GOOD—Numismatic term for coin in somewhat worn condition, but with date and inscription still sharp and clear.

GRAIN—Unit of English system of weights; 1/7000 of a pound.

GREENBACK—U.S. paper money with back printed in green.

GROAT—Old English silver coin worth fourpence.

GUILDER—English term for Dutch gulden.

GUINEA—Seventeenth, eighteenth, and early nineteenth century English gold coin worth from 20 to 30 shillings. Term is still used in England as "money of account."

GULDEN—Dutch silver coin; standard monetary unit of The Netherlands.

HALF CENT—U.S. copper coin issued irregularly, 1793 through 1857.

HALF DIME—U.S. silver coin issued irregularly, 1794 through 1804 and 1829 through 1873.

HALF-DOLLAR—U.S. silver coin issued in all but eight years since 1794.

HALF EAGLE—U.S. $5 gold piece, issued 1795–1916 in all but two years, and for the single year of 1929.

HALFPENNY—English coin of half a penny's value.

HARD TIMES TOKENS—Metal pieces resembling coins, issued privately in U.S., 1832–44, for circulation to replace scarce government specie. Most of them bore advertisements or political slogans.

HEADS—Slang for *obverse* of coin.

HOGGE MONEY—Popular name for coins with hog device, issued in Sommer Islands (now Bermuda), 1616–24.

HOLED COIN—A coin mutilated by a hole drilled through it.

INCUSE—Sunken design on coin; opposite of *relief*.

INDIAN HEAD—U.S. copper-cent type 1859–1909. Indian heads also have appeared on five-cent pieces and on gold eagles, half eagles, and quarter eagles.

INGOT—Metal mass cast into a mold before being cut into coins.

INSCRIPTION—A coin's legend or lettering, including numerals.

INTAGLIO—Engraving in which design is hollowed out; not raised. (Opposite of *relief*.)

JEFFERSON NICKEL—Five-cent piece bearing Thomas Jefferson's bust on obverse.

JOACHIMSTHALER—Early sixteenth century silver coin (first made in St. Joachimsdale, Bohemia) on which Spanish and U.S. dollars were modeled.

JOE—Slang term for *johannes*, an eighteenth century Portuguese gold coin often used in the Colonies.

JUGATE—Same as *conjoined*.

KENNEDY HALF-DOLLAR—U.S. silver fifty-cent piece with bust of John F. Kennedy on obverse; issued since 1964.

L or £—Common abbreviation for English pound.

LARGE CENT—U.S. copper one-cent piece of 1-inch to 1-1/8-inch diameter, issued 1793–1857 (except 1815).

LAUREATED—Crowned with laurel wreath.

LEGAL TENDER—Currency which may not legally be refused in payment of indebtedness.

LEGEND—Wording or letters on a coin.

LEPTON—Smallest copper coin of ancient Greece and other Mediterranean countries—the *mite* of the New Testament.

LETTERED EDGE—Inscription around a coin's vertical edge.

LEVANT DOLLAR—See *Maria Theresa dollar*.

LIBERTY—Symbolical representation of Goddess of Liberty used on many U.S. coins. Types include Liberty Bust, Liberty Cap, Liberty Head, Liberty Seated, Liberty Standing, and Liberty Walking.

LINCOLN PENNY—U.S. cent bearing bust of Abraham Lincoln, issued since 1909.

LIRA—Monetary unit of Italy.

LORD BALTIMORE COINS—Shillings, sixpence, groats, and pennies struck in England in 1659 by Cecil, Lord Baltimore, for use in his Maryland "plantation."

LOUIS D'OR—Gold coin of France from 1640 until French Revolution; popularly known as *pistole*.

MARIA THERESA DOLLAR—Modern copy of 1780 Austrian

thaler, bearing head of Empress Maria Theresa and 1780 date. It is still made in several European mints for use in eastern Mediterranean countries distrusting modern coinage. Also called *Levant dollar*.

MARKET VALUE—Price at which a collector can buy.

MATTE PROOF—Proof coin with dull finish.

MAUNDY MONEY—Series of four small coins, from penny to fourpence, struck each year in Great Britain for giving to poor persons as Royal Bounty on Maundy Thursday (Thursday before Easter).

MEDAL—Metal disk resembling a coin, but not legal tender, with device and inscription commemorating a notable person or occasion.

MERCURY-HEAD DIME—Popular name for 1916–54 dime bearing winged Liberty head.

MEXICAN DOLLAR—Common term for Mexican or South American peso, especially when used for trade in Far East.

MILL—Term used in accounting: one tenth of U.S. cent.

MILLED EDGE or MILLING—Rim raised above surface at coin's edge.

MILLED MONEY—Coins produced by screw press.

MINT—Place where money is coined.

MINT CONDITION—Same as *uncirculated*.

MINT ERROR—Same as *freak*.

MINT MARK—Letter stamped on coin to indicate where it was struck.

MINT SET—Specimens of all types of coins struck in all U.S. mints in one year.

MINT STATE—Same as *uncirculated*.

MISSTRIKE—Coin that has been struck crooked or off center.

MITE—Any small coin of little value.

MODULE—Diameter of a coin.

MONEY—Any form of currency lawfully used as a medium of exchange.

MONEYER—An authorized mintmaster or coin maker.

MONEY OF ACCOUNT—Monetary unit in which accounts are stated, such as British *pound sterling*, French *franc*, or U.S. *dollar*.

MORGAN HEAD DOLLAR—Common numismatic name for 1878–1921 Liberty head dollar designed by mint engraver George T. Morgan.

MOTTO—Inscription containing words of guidance or inspiration.

MULE—A "mixed-up" coin, with obverse and reverse struck from dies of different issues.

MUTILATED COIN—A piece that has lost its numismatic and sometimes its face value through being tampered with (holed, plugged, cut, nicked, flattened, etc.)

NAPOLEON—Nineteenth century French gold coin, worth 20 francs.

NEW ENGLAND (or NE) MONEY—First money coined in North American Colonies: shilling, sixpence, and threepenny pieces minted in Massachusetts Bay Colony in 1652.

NICKEL—Common name of U.S. five-cent piece, containing copper and nickel; issued in all but four years since 1866.

NUMISMATICS—Science or study of coins, tokens, medals, paper money, and other mediums of exchange.

NUMISMATIST—Person specializing in numismatics.

OAK TREE COINS—Silver shillings, sixpence, threepence, and twopence with oak tree device, issued by Massachusetts Bay Colony 1658–67, but mostly bearing 1652 date.

OBVERSE—Face of coin, usually containing date and main design. (Often called *heads*.)

OVERDATE—Coin struck from die on which date has been changed to replace an earlier year with a later one.

OVERSTRIKE—A new impression made on an old coin.

OXIDATION—Darkening of a coin's surface, caused by exposure to air or chemicals.

PAPER MONEY—Legal-tender paper currency issued by governments or banks.

PATINA—Coating (usually greenish) found on old copper coins.

PATTERN COIN—Experimental piece, struck to demonstrate proposed new design.

PEACE DOLLAR—U.S. silver dollar issued 1921–28 and 1934–35 to mark conclusion of World War I.

PENNY—English coin worth 1/12 shilling, or slightly more than U.S. cent; originally silver, later copper, now bronze. Also common term for *cent* in U.S.

PESETA—Old Spanish coin worth two reales, or one-fourth dollar.

PESO—Spanish or Mexican dollar.

PIASTRE—Common term for Spanish *peso*. Also the standard unit of coinage in Turkey, Egypt, and several other Mediterranean countries.

PIECE OF EIGHT—Spanish dollar, used by colonists in all parts of North and South America and often cut into eight pieces or *bits* for small change.

PILLAR DOLLAR—Common name for 1732–71 Spanish dollar with two tall pillars on reverse.

PINE TREE COINS—Silver shillings, sixpence, and threepence with pine tree device, struck by Massachusetts Bay Colony 1667–82, but all bearing 1652 date.

PISTOLE—Popular French name for sixteenth–seventeenth century Spanish double escudo and for seventeenth–eighteenth century French louis d'or.

PLANCHET—Blank metal disk on which coin is stamped. (Same as *blank* or *flan*.)

PLUGGED COIN—Coin with a drilled hole that has been filled with metal in attempt to hide it.

POLE—Stick over Liberty's shoulder, holding her cap, on some 1793, '94, and '95 half cents and cents.

POOR—Term describing coin in such bad condition that legend and design are partly worn away.

POUND SOVEREIGN—Same as *sovereign*.

POUND STERLING—The British monetary unit, worth 20 shillings, or $2.80 in U.S. money.

PREMIUM VALUE—Money paid or received for a coin over face value.

PRIVATE GOLD—Gold coins or slugs issued privately or by state, territorial, or local governments.

PROOF—Coin with bright, mirror-like finish, struck on polished blank.

PYX—Special chest in which a mint keeps specimen coins reserved for tests of weight or fineness.

QUARTER—U.S. silver or silver-alloy 25-cent piece, issued irregularly 1796–1830 and in all but three years since 1831.

QUARTER EAGLE—U.S. $2.50 gold piece, issued irregularly 1796–1827 and regularly 1829–1915 and 1925–29.

QUARTO—Same as *cuarto*.

RAISED—Standing above a coin's general level. (Opposite of *recessed*.)

REALE or REAL—Former silver monetary unit of Spain and Latin America, worth 1/8 peso or 12-1/2 cents in U.S. money; often called a *bit*.

RECESSED—Indented. (Opposite of *raised*.)

RECUT DATE—Coin made from die on which a numeral or letter has been repunched to correct a poor impression.

REEDED EDGE—Coin edge with parallel vertical ridges to discourage trimming of metal.

RELIEF—Portion of design above surface level. (Opposite of *incuse*.)

RESTRIKE—Coin struck at later date than original coins from same die.

REVERSE—Back side of coin, commonly called *tails*.

RIM—Raised border or margin on coin.

ROLL—Paper-wrapped, cylindrical package of new coins of one date, denomination, and design, all from one mint.

ROOSEVELT DIME—U.S. ten-cent silver piece bearing bust of Franklin D. Roosevelt, issued since 1946.

ROSA AMERICANA—Series of twopenny, penny, and half-penny copper-and-zinc coins featuring a rose, struck in England 1722–24 for use of North American colonists.

RUBBING—Method of copying a coin's design by covering it with moist tracing paper and rubbing it first with fingers and then with soft pencil.

s.—Abbreviation for *shilling*.

SAINT PATRICK'S MONEY—Halfpennies and farthings displaying likeness of Saint Patrick, struck in Dublin in seventeenth century and used as legal currency in New Jersey.

SCREW PRESS—Press which stamps coins by turning a spindle that forces a metal ram down upon a blank.

SCRIP—Paper document of stated monetary value, issued in place of official government currency and sometimes used instead of money in times of emergency.

SERIES—Specimens from all mints of a single design of coin of each date.

SHIELD-TYPE NICKEL—U.S. 1866–83 five-cent piece, with shield on face.

SHILLING—English silver coin worth 12 pence. Formerly roughly equal to U.S. quarter, but now only 14 cents.

SHINPLASTER—Formerly common slang term for early U.S. paper money.

SIGNATURE—Small initial or initials appearing on a coin to identify its designer.

SILVER DOLLAR—Large U.S. silver coin issued irregularly 1793–1935. See *dollar*.

SIXPENCE—English silver coin worth half a shilling.

SLUG—Lump of refined gold worth $50, privately issued in California during the gold rush.

SMALL CENT—U.S. one-cent piece since 1856 (so called to distinguish it from earlier *large cent*).

SOL—See *sou*.

SOU (formerly *sol*)—French five-centime piece, worth 1/20 franc.

SOVEREIGN—Large English gold coin worth 20 shillings, no longer issued. (Same as *pound sovereign*).

SPECIE—Money made of metal, as distinguished from paper money.

STATE COINAGE—Coins issued by individual states after the Revolution and before U.S. Mint began producing national coinage.

STELLA—Rare experimental $4 gold piece struck in 1879–80, bearing large five-pointed star on reverse.

STERLING—Term indicating that a coin is of standard value or purity.

STIVER—Small Dutch coin of billon or copper widely used in Dutch overseas possessions in colonial times.

STRIKE—To impress a metal blank with a die or dies, making a coin.

STUIVER—Same as *stiver*.

SUBSIDIARY COINS—Coins of value less than a dollar.

SYMBOL—Subordinate design on a coin.

TALER—Same as *thaler*.

TERRITORIAL GOLD—See *private gold*.

TETRADRACHM—Ancient Greek silver coin.

THALER—Large silver Germanic coin from which U.S. dollar got its name. Same as *taler*.

THREE-CENT NICKEL—U.S. coin of nickel, copper, and zinc, issued 1865–89 (except 1877).

THREE-CENT SILVER PIECE—Smallest size coin ever issued by U.S.; struck 1851–73.

THREE DOLLAR GOLD PIECE—U.S. coin issued 1854–89.

THREEPENCE—British silver coin worth three pennies.

TOKEN—A piece of metal accepted as currency, usually issued privately when official coinage is scarce.

TOKEN COINAGE—Coins whose real value is less than their face value.

TRADE DOLLAR—Large U.S. silver coin of a dollar's value, issued especially for trade in the Orient.

TRANSITIONAL PATTERN—Coin having features of both old and new designs, issued while pattern is being changed.

TREASURY NOTE—Paper money issued by U.S. Treasury.

TREE MONEY—Coins with willow, oak, or pine tree device, struck in Massachusetts from 1652 to 1682, but nearly all bearing 1652 date.

TRIAL OF THE PYX—Annual test of U.S. coins' fineness and weight made at the mint by special commissioners who examine specimen coins reserved in special chest or *pyx*.

TRIAL PIECES—Impressions made on soft metal to test new dies.

TRIME—Once-popular name for U.S. silver three-cent piece, coined 1851–73.

TRUNCATION—Line at base of neck where bust on a coin is usually cut off.

TWENTY-CENT PIECE—U.S. silver coin issued 1875–78.

TWO BITS—Slang term for 25 cents, derived from the 12-1/2-cent *bits* of Spanish *pieces of eight*.

TWO-CENT PIECE—U.S. bronze coin, issued 1864–73.

TYPE—Distinguishing design of a coin.

TYPE-COLLECTING—Collecting one coin of each type, but of any date or mint.

TYPE SET—A group of coins including one of each design, but not of each mint or date.

UNCIRCULATED—A coin showing no signs of wear—as fresh as if just minted. (Same as *mint condition*.)

UPGRADING—Replacing coins in a collection with others of superior condition.

VDB—Initials of mint designer Victor D. Brenner, appearing on early 1909 Lincoln cents and on all since 1918.

WAMPUM—Beads made of seashells, used as money by North American Indians and also by some colonists.

WASHINGTON COINS—Numerous types of cents, half pennies, pennies, and half-dollars bearing name and likeness of George Washington, issued by various sources, mostly in England, from 1783 to 1795.

WASHINGTON QUARTER—U.S. 25-cent piece since 1932, with bust of George Washington on obverse.

WIDOW'S MITE—New Testament term for coin of small value, generally believed to refer to Greek or Judean lepton.

WILLOW TREE COINS—Shillings, sixpence, and three pence with willow tree device, struck in Massachusetts from 1653 to 1658 or '60, but all bearing 1652 date.

WINGED-HEAD DIME—U.S. 1916–45 ten-cent piece, popularly known as *Mercury dime*.

WIRE EDGE—Exceptionally sharp rim around a coin.

WOOD'S COINAGE—Copper halfpenny and farthing dated 1722 to 1724, designed in England by William Wood for use in Ireland, but so unpopular there that they were sent to American Colonies instead.

COIN DISPLAYS

Among the best exhibits of coins are those at the American Numismatic Society Museum, the Chase Manhattan Bank Money

Museum, and the Metropolitan Museum, all in New York City; the Smithsonian Institution and Dumbarton Oaks, both in Washington, D.C.; the U.S. Mint in Philadelphia; the Fogg Art Museum at Harvard University, Cambridge, Mass., the Museum of Fine Arts, Boston, Mass.; the Buffalo Museum of Science, Buffalo, N.Y.; Princeton Library, Princeton, N.J.; Yale University, New Haven, Conn.; Omaha Public Library, Omaha, Neb.; National Bank of Detroit, Detroit, Mich.; Republic National Bank, Dallas, Tex.; First National Bank, Chicago, Ill.; First National Bank, Minneapolis, Minn.; and a number of other art museums, libraries, and banks.

INDEX

DATE DUE

DE 17'76		
MR 23'77		
MY 26'77		
OC 13'77		
NO 23'77		
OC 31'79		
NO 2 '83		
AP 15'84		
NOV 4 1985		
MR 23'92		